I0828328

Wicked ANN ARBOR

JAMES THOMAS MANN

Published by The History Press
Charleston, SC 29403
www.historypress.net

First published 2011

978-1-5402-3053-9

Library of Congress Cataloging-in-Publication Data

Mann, James Thomas.
Wicked Ann Arbor / James Thomas Mann.
p. cm.
Includes bibliographical references.
ISBN 978-1-5402-3053-9
1. Ann Arbor (Mich.)--History--Anecdotes. 2. Ann Arbor (Mich.)--Social life and customs--Anecdotes. 3. Ann Arbor (Mich.)--Biography--Anecdotes. 4. Violence--Michigan--Ann Arbor--History--Anecdotes. 5. Death--Michigan--Ann Arbor--History--Anecdotes. 6. Curiosities and wonders--Michigan--Ann Arbor--History--Anecdotes. I. Title.
F574.A6M34 2011
977.4'35--dc23
2011034749

Contents

Acknowledgements

I wish to express my gratitude to those whose help made this work possible: George Ridenour, who helped with the research and found the missing but important facts; Al Rudisill, president of the Ypsilanti Historical Society, who helped with the images; and the staff of the Bentley Library, University of Michigan, for all the help they provided. Once again, I am thankful for all the help I received from the student workers at the University of Michigan Grad Library microfilm room, as they solved all the new problems I discovered while using the equipment.

1

Dangers of Drink

Ann Arbor is a city that has enjoyed a history of low crime and few acts of violence. What trouble that has occurred over the years has often been the result of drinking. Those who drink beyond their limits risk indulging in wild and reckless acts that sometimes result in injury and even murder. Here are a few examples of such acts that were the result of drink.

Probable Murder

Someone had a bad start to the day on the morning of Wednesday, November 6, 1861. On that morning, at about 6:00 a.m., someone made the unpleasant discovery of a dead body on Main Street, in front of the store of Maynard, Stebbins & Wilson. This caused considerable excitement in the city of Ann Arbor. The city marshal, Mr. O.M. Martin, was immediately informed and came at once to examine the body. He found the body to be quite warm. There were also considerable pools of blood on the stone doorsill and on the planking of the walk. The blood was from a wound about an inch and a half long on the victim's left temple, penetrating to the bone. A Dr. Lewitt, upon examination of the body, determined that the wound had been inflicted by some blunt instrument, which had severed a small artery. Dr. Lewitt would testify that the wound was likely caused by a narrow, dull hatchet or, more probably, by the edge of a board or club. Death was caused by concussion.

City Marshal Martin examined the body and ascertained that it belonged to John Innis, an Irishman who was well known to many residents of Ann Arbor. He had lived in the county and the city for the previous twenty-five years. "Innis," reported the *Michigan Argus* of Friday, November 8, 1861, "is generally spoken of as a quiet, peaceable, inoffensive man, without enemies, though one enemy, a bottle of whiskey, was found with him." In the pocket of his pantaloons was found his wallet, containing a note for $180, and in his coat pocket was a pint bottle of whiskey.

Justice of the peace C.H. Vaneleve impaneled a jury for an inquest. The jurors heard testimony on November 6 and 8. Innis had spent the summer working on a farm in either Northfield or Salem Township and had spent the previous weeks on a spree. On the night of his death, Innis had left the grocery story of Edward Earl, on Ann Street, at about 10:00 p.m. He was in the company of Barnard Harkins, and both were very much intoxicated. The two left the store in search of lodging for the night. As they walked past the store of Maynard, Stebbins & Wilson, Innis fell and struck his head on some hard substance. This caused the wound that led to his death between the hours of one and six o'clock in the morning.

All but one of the jurors agreed with this verdict. Ransom S. Smith dissented. He held the opinion that Innis's death was caused by a blow from a stick or cane in the hands of some person.

DEATH OF O'BRIEN

Charles Patterson was the editor of the *Ypsilanti Commercial*, as well as an ardent prohibitionist who condemned drinking and the sale of alcoholic beverages. On the evening of Saturday, October 9, 1869, Patterson once again denounced drunkenness and licentiousness, stating, "These joint evils are largely on the increase in our midst. Drunken men are almost daily committed to the lock up. A terrible pity that the rum seller could not be chained to his victim and both together be consigned to durance vile. Many of our young men are on the road to ruin. Drink and bad associations are rendering them vile and brutal."

The night before, on Friday, October 8, 1869, three young men had boarded the train at Ypsilanti and rode into Ann Arbor. The three were George Knisely, Arthur Crich and John Walker. At Ann Arbor, the trio visited several saloons and were joined by William O'Brien. O'Brien was nineteen years old and was said to have been a peaceable young man. At the Exchange Hotel, O'Brien and Knisely got into an altercation, during which O'Brien knocked Knisely down. Knisely arose and laughed it off, then treated the others to a round of drinks. Soon after, however, Knisely was heard to say something about killing the man who had knocked him down.

Knisely and O'Brien, with Crich and Walker, left the Exchange Hotel at about 10:00 p.m. and began walking toward the Michigan Central Depot. Near Detroit Street, Crich and Walker left the other two, and by 12:30 a.m., they had engaged rooms at the Cook's Hotel, where they spent the night.

"About 11 o'clock the lamp lighter in going his rounds to turn off the gas, saw the body of a man lying near the corner of Huron and Fifth Streets, but did not stop, as he supposed the man to be intoxicated," reported the *Detroit Free Press* of Wednesday, October 13, 1869.

Just before 6:00 a.m., an omnibus driver found the body on the street and went to summon a Dr. Smith. When found, the body was lying on its back with its coat off and the right arm cut nearly off. The body was taken to the nearby engine house, where an examination of the wounds was made. A stab wound was found in the left breast, near the heart.

Early that morning, before the discovery of the body, Knisely had gone to the Michigan Central Depot and asked the men there to drink with him. There, he made a remark about having "cut the heart out of a man last night." He also said something about how he had to "keep scarce." No one present took the comment seriously, as it was thought he was indulging in drunken bragging. He was quite drunk at the time. He, along with Crich and Walker, took the early train back to Ypsilanti.

That same day, all three were arrested under suspicion and returned to Ann Arbor. "When Knisely was arrested, blood was found upon his shirt bosom, pocket handkerchief and pants," noted the *Detroit Free Press.*

That same morning, someone passing the site where the body had been found came across a large jackknife with a blade about four inches long. The knife had been sharpened on both sides of the point. The knife was recognized as belonging to George Knisely. No trace of blood, however, was found on the knife. "It is reported that Knisely sharpened his knife Friday morning and made some taunting threats," noted the *Ypsilanti Commercial* of Saturday, October 15, 1869.

An inquest was held on Monday, October 11, 1869, and rendered a verdict that William O'Brien had died by means of a stab wound inflicted by George Knisely. After the verdict was rendered, Knisely confessed to the murder, and Crich and Walker were released.

"Much excitement prevails among the Irish citizens and fears are entertained that an effort will be made to-night to lynch the prisoner," concluded the *Detroit Free Press.*

There were reasons for the fear. At one point, as the crowd pressed forward, a deputy sheriff stood with a pistol in each hand and assured the crowd that they would have to pass over his dead body to get at Knisely. That night, the jail was in the charge of a unit of the local militia, but no further disturbance occurred.

Knisely stood trial at the October term of the circuit court and was found guilty and sentenced to eight years in the state prison.

"This murder business is the strongest sermon against the ungodly business of liquor selling that can be preached," thundered Patterson in the next issue of the *Ypsilanti Commercial.* "The next giant evil against which all good men in this land must *unite* and put down by the omnipotent power of moral sentiment, by the silent, and all persuasive power of the ballot, by *law enforced* by public opinion, and if need be a million bayonets, is the liquor traffic. No problem can be more clearly demonstrated than that the American people must annihilate the liquor traffic or be annihilated by it."

SHOOTING AFFRAY

On the evening of Friday, October 28, 1870, some friends were sitting in Hangsterfer's Saloon. Between the hours of ten and eleven o'clock, just after the close of the theatrical performance in the hall above and before the start of a dance that had been advertised for that evening, some medical students from the university entered. They had already been drinking and came into the saloon seeking more refreshments. One of the students noticed Andrew Duncan. Duncan clearly had had enough to drink and was sitting in a chair with his head on the table. The student, perhaps thinking it would be funny, pulled the chair away, and Duncan fell to the floor. At this, John Kean, a clerk in the store of E. Duffy, remarked that no gentleman would do that.

The student was not pleased with this remark and exchanged words with Kean. The two scuffled and were pulled apart. Just then, a second student, named Henry Johnson, stepped forward and drew a revolver. Someone pulled Johnson's arm as he pulled the trigger, and the shot went into the wall. Johnson fired a second time; this time, the shot struck Kean in the right breast. The bullet may have lodged in his lung.

In the excitement of the moment, Johnson made his escape. For some reason, the authorities were not informed of the shooting until the next morning.

"Johnson fled into the country," reported the *Michigan Argus* of Friday, November 4, 1870, "stopped at a farm-house in Superior [Township] about 3 o'clock a.m., reporting himself thrown from a horse, stayed until morning, left about 6 o'clock, went to Ypsilanti, jumped on the 11 a.m. freight train after it left the station, and arrived at Detroit about 2 o'clock P.M., since which no trace has been discovered."

"Previous to going to Hangsterfer's," continued the *Michigan Argus*, "reports say he visited Binder's, kicked up a disturbance there, and knocked his man down with a billiard cue."

Henry C. Johnson Jr. was the son of a prominent lawyer of Meadville, Pennsylvania. He had been in Ann Arbor only a few weeks, as he had recently resigned a lieutenant's commission in the regular army.

The authorities issued a circular in the hope of finding Johnson:

> *500 REWARD*
>
> *On the night of October 28, 1870, one Henry C. Johnson, Jr., shot a citizen of Ann Arbor, Mich. Johnson is about 23 years old; 5 feet 8 inches in height; weight, 150 pounds; light complexion, blue eyes (watery) appearance; brown hair; had light side whiskers; was dressed in dark shirt and light pants, and alpaca cap. Is from Meadville, Pa., where his father resides. Has been in the army several years. He is slow of speech.*
>
> *I will pay $200 for his apprehension and conviction.*

W. D. HARRIMAN,
Mayor, City of Ann Arbor, Mich.
I will pay $300 when convicted
BYRON R. PORTER,
Sheriff, Washtenaw Co., Mich.
Address BYRON R. PORTER Sheriff,
Ann Arbor, Mich.

Kean, noted the *Michigan Argus*, was a steady, sober and industrious young man, the victim of an unprovoked attack, as he and Johnson had not exchanged a single word and Johnson's friend was in no danger. Doctors expressed fears that Kean would not recover from the wound.

"Is it not time," stated the *Michigan Argus*, "that the rules of the University prohibited students carrying fire-arms, and that expulsion was visited on the heads of every offender. And if a single drunken spree brought expulsion, or even the habitual frequenting of drinking saloons, we should not complain."

Nothing more was heard of Johnson until Wednesday, November 16, when, on that morning, his father delivered him to the authorities in Detroit. He was then taken to Ann Arbor and lodged in the jail there. "He would have been brought here before," noted the *Peninsular Courier* of Friday, November 4, 1870, "only that his mother was lying at the point of death, and is still in a very critical situation. His father is willing to settle the matter if he can do so honorably, otherwise he says the law must take its course."

That same day, the *Michigan Argus* reported that Kean was doing well.

The case came before the circuit court during the term of March 1871. When the case came to trial, the prosecution withdrew the charge of assault with intent to murder and entered the charge of assault and battery. Johnson withdrew his plea of not guilty and entered a plea of guilty to the charge of assault and battery. The *Peninsular Courier* reported on March 10, 1871, that Johnson was fined ten dollars, "paid the costs of prosecution and settled the matter with Kean." The terms of the settlement were not reported.

Fatal Row at Flannary's Saloon

Richard Flannary was said to have been a quiet and inoffensive man. He was the proprietor of a saloon on the southwest corner of Main and Catharine Streets in Ann Arbor. Flannary was in the saloon business only a short time, as a fatal row broke out in his place on the night of Friday, October 30, 1874.

On that Friday evening, Charles Holiday was in the saloon, as were Joseph Audett, Hiram Pickard, Peter Hanlon and John Norton, as well as two African American men and two strangers. Pickard was drunk and was described as "hopping around." For no reason, Pickard struck one of the strangers in the face. Richard Flannary and Charles Holiday told Pickard, "It was too bad to strike a man that way." At this, Pickard walked up to the stranger, shook hands with him and begged his pardon. Then he walked away.

Not long after this, Pickard told Peter Hanlon to pay Flannary the ten cents he owed the proprietor. Hanlon said he did not owe Flannary anything. Pickard then knocked Hanlon down. Flannary told Pickard to leave the saloon. Pickard told Flannary he would go when he was ready. Flannary placed his hand on Pickard's collar and said, "You must go now."

Pickard resisted Flannary's efforts to put him out. John Flannary, Richard's brother, came to help Richard. The two were able to get Pickard between the screen and the door. Then, Jethro Maybe jumped to his feet. Charles Holiday told Maybe to leave them alone. Maybe grabbed John Flannary and pulled him off Pickard, leaving Pickard in the hands of Richard. Holiday took hold of Maybe and pulled him off John Flannary. Maybe picked up a chair. Holiday told Maybe, "Don't strike me with that."

Instead, Maybe dodged around and behind the stove, and when he was near Richard Flannary, he raised the chair and struck the man a tremendous blow on the top of his head. Flannary fell to the floor senseless.

Richard Flannary was taken to his home, where a Dr. Smith was summoned. Dr. Smith was called for again early on Saturday morning and found Richard Flannary in a comatose condition. Flannary remained in a comatose condition until his death.

Coroner Breaky and Prosecuting Attorney Allen held an inquest on the following Monday. Charles Holiday was the first witness. He and the other witnesses testified to having seen Maybe strike Richard Flannary. Dr. Smith reported on the postmortem examination he had made: "In my opinion the fracture of the skull and the resulting hemorrhage and pressure upon the brain by the clot caused death." A Dr. Leiter, who had assisted in the postmortem examination, corroborated the testimony of Dr. Smith.

The jury of the inquest then rendered its verdict: "That the deceased, Richard Flannary, came to his death by a blow from a chair in the hands of Jethro Maybe, on the night of Friday, the 30th of October, and further that Hiram Pickard was present and assisted, aided and abetted in the assault."

Maybe stood trial in September 1875 and was found guilty of manslaughter. He was sentenced to the state prison for one year.

2
Double Murder

The first public building to be erected in Washtenaw County was the jail, constructed in about 1829. This was made of timber and was a rude affair with room for the jailer in the front and a single cell in the back. A second jail was built in 1837. It was made of brick and was two and a half stories high. In the front of the building were rooms for the jailer and in the rear were apartments and cells for the prisoners. Prisoners were not the only ones who spent the night in the cells; travelers and others who had no place to stay were allowed to spend the night there. This was a practice that continued into the twentieth century. Such a request was made on the night of Sunday, October 22, 1871.

At about midnight, Henry Wagner came running down the street, appearing excited and looking anxiously behind him. Wagner asked the jailer if he could spend the night, and the jailer admitted Wagner and locked him in a cell. There, Wagner spent a restless night without falling asleep. In the morning, the jailer released him. As Wagner was leaving, he burst out crying but did not explain the reason for his feelings.

From the jail, Wagner went uptown, where he met his brother, August. He said to his brother, "I don't know what I have been doing. I don't know whether she will live or not." Henry Wagner then told his brother that he had murdered his wife, Henrietta.

The two then went to the house of a Mrs. Schlotterbeck, who ran a saloon on Main Street, and turned over to her the key to the house where Henry Wagner and his wife had lived. They told her to give the key to a Mr. Rettich, who owned the building. Wagner then confessed to her that he had murdered his wife. Henry Wagner told Mrs. Schlotterbeck that he had not intended to kill his wife. He claimed that when he struck her, she had clasped her hands and cried out, "Oh, my God, I am killed," then she fell to the floor.

At about 7:00 a.m., Mr. Rettich turned the key over to Officer Thomas Leonard and told him to go to Mrs. Wagner's store, as Mr. Wagner had murdered his wife. Officer Leonard went at once to the Wagners' house. This was on Washington Street. In the front of the house, Mrs. Wagner ran a fancy goods store, and in the rear was a sleeping apartment for the family. Officer Leonard unlocked the door and went inside.

According to the *Peninsular Courier* of October 27, 1871:

> *A spectacle met his eye that nearly froze his blood. In the room in the rear of the store, which was occupied by the deceased and Wagner as their living room, and in which was their bed, at the side of the bed lay Mrs. Wagner in her night dress, lying on her right side, her feet extended under the bed a short distance; one arm was under her and the other thrown over and upward toward her head; her head was one mass of pounded flesh and bone; from it had flowed half a gallon of blood; around her were spatters of blood, and clots of bloody gore covered her night cloths. Near her head lay the murderous weapon, a common hatchet, and that too was stained with blood.*

Leonard had been in the room about ten minutes, almost paralyzed by the sight, when he heard a gurgling sound from the bed. He raised the covering to find Oscar, the three-year-old son of Mrs. Wagner and the stepson of Henry. Oscar's head had been pounded in the same manner as his mother's, but he was still alive, having, as noted by the *Michigan Argus* of Friday, October 27, 1871, "laid there and wallowed in its own blood for over eight hours."

A Dr. Cheever arrived on the scene soon after and told Officer Leonard that the child could not live. Oscar was removed from the site and died a few hours later.

"Coroner Peek was notified and took charge of the bodies. An excited crowd soon gathered around the building, and threats of lynching were made," noted the *Peninsular Courier*.

At the jail, a reporter for the *Free Press* interviewed Wagner, who made a statement that was published by both the *Peninsular Courier* and the *Michigan Argus*:

> *I have had some trouble with my wife and we have had several quarrels. Once when I accidentally threw some wash water on the boy, she came at me and caught me by the hair, called me a dog, and told me to leave the house and never be seen there again. Notwithstanding these differences, I have always loved my wife very dearly.*
>
> *For the past two or three days we have lived most happily; she never seemed to love me so much. Last night she went to bed, I don't know at what time. I said to her good night, and went to the bed to kiss her, when she spit in my face and kicked at me saying, go away, you are a crazy man, and I can't live with a crazy man. I said to her, give me my money and I will go. She said nothing to this. I then went and got the money and started to leave, when she jumped up and said, I will cut you in pieces before you go with that money. That made me very angry, and I took the hatchet from the woodbox and went toward her, she jumped at me and called me a dog and told me to leave the house. I kept brandishing the hatchet to frighten her. She and the child both cried fire and murder, and as she clutched me by the throat I hit her accidentally. She fell right down and said: "O, my," and groaned. When I saw what I had done, that she was hurt so she could never get well, I thought I would put an end to her life, and struck her several times. After this I remember nothing. I seemed to see my wife before my eyes all the time. I don't remember striking the boy at all. I only remember putting out the light and locking the door. I went out in the street, but I could not go anywhere where I did not see my wife just as I struck her, lying before my eyes. I came down to the jail but I could not sleep or eat. I don't know what I shall do!*

The reporter noted that Wagner often stopped to cry and seemed very much excited; he said he would give anything not to have done it. "He manifestly knows something about the insanity game," noted the reporter, "for he spoke several times, saying his brain runs all in a whirl, and that he must be crazy. He said he did not expect to get free, but expected to suffer the full penalty of the law."

When Wagner arrived at the jail the second time, he had $100 with him. "Wagner has considerable money—about three thousand dollars—a part of which is still in Germany," noted the *Peninsular Courier*. "A short time ago he made a contract, giving her [his wife] the whole of it. This contract was found in the morning in his coat pocket, torn in two. By some it is supposed that he murdered her to get possession of the money again, having repented of his former generosity." The inquest was held the afternoon of the same day as the bodies were found.

At the inquest, a Mary Miley testified. She was a partner in the business of the fancy goods shop. She and Henrietta Wagner had gone into business on June 1. She said that Henry Wagner often came to the shop to see Henrietta. Henry told Mary he was Henrietta's brother-in-law. The two were married on July 17 and lived together in the back of the store. "About two weeks after they were married, they commenced having trouble. He was jealous of her. At one time when they had a difficulty, she threatened to throw the lamp at him. After the difficulty, he went away, but came back in about a week. He called her bad names and said she had never been married to his brother."

Mary said she had seen Henry Wagner on the night of the murder, at about 7:30 p.m. "He said he loved his wife and thought everything of her but that she lied to him and was cross, that he had willed her all his property, including the money yet to come from Germany, but that she did not treat him well. He said she was not his brother's wife, and never had been married to him or divorced from him. Jealousy was the first cause of their trouble."

On Monday, Henrietta was to go to Detroit to purchase goods for the shop, and Mary was to tend to the shop while she was away. Henry told Mary that Henrietta was not well enough to make the trip. Mary, Henry told her, did not need to come to the shop on Monday morning.

Henry told Mary that Henrietta had told him the week before "that she did not care if he did leave, that she had all his money."

August Wagner, the brother of Henry, testified as well. "There was great trouble between the deceased and my brother about this child," he said. "She had been the prostitute of my oldest brother in Germany for four or five years. He used to say they were married. They had several children. My oldest brother wrote to the deceased that he believed this child was a child of his own brother."

The surgeons testified that there were six wounds on the head; the largest was about two and a half inches in length, and the brain was protruding from the wound. "All were probably caused by the blunt end of the hatchet. She was probably struck while sitting on the bed."

The jury returned a verdict:

> *Henrietta Wagner, late of the city of Ann Arbor came to her death on the night of October 22nd, 1871, by blows inflicted upon her head by a certain hatchet in the hands of Henry Wagner. Said blows were inflicted upon the said Henrietta Wagner by the said Henry Wagner, feloniously; willfully and of his malice aforethought with intent her, the said Henrietta Wagner, to kill and murder.*

The jury returned the same verdict in regard to the child, Oscar Wagner.

The case of Henry Wagner came to trial in March 1872, and the defense did not contest the main facts. The defense admitted that Henrietta Wagner had been killed by Henry Wagner at the time and place charged. Henry's defense was insanity. The jury was out for two hours and returned with a verdict of "guilty of murder in the first degree." Henry was sentenced to solitary confinement and hard labor for life. He was then taken to the prison in Jackson.

According to Samuel Beakes in *Past and Present of Washtenaw County, Michigan*, Henry Wagner became "violently insane and in 1887 was sent to the criminal asylum for the insane."

3

Defalcation at the University

The Douglas-Rose Controversy

Dr. Silas H. Douglas was, by 1875, one of the most prominent members of the faculty of the university, as well as the city, of Ann Arbor. No one would have guessed it at that time, but he was soon to be embroiled in what was perhaps the most serious controversy in the history of the University of Michigan. This was the Douglas-Rose Controversy, the ill effects of which were still felt as late as the 1940s.

Douglas was born in Fredonia, Chautauqua County, New York, on October 27, 1816. He studied at Fredonia Academy and graduated from the University of Vermont, from which he received the degree of master of arts. He moved to Michigan in 1838 and settled in Detroit, where he studied medicine under Drs. Rice and Pitcher and earned his MD at the University of Maryland. He returned to Michigan and was a member of the geological survey under Douglas Houghton. Later, he was physician to a party, under Henry R. Schoolcraft, engaged in negotiating treaties with Native Americans. Douglas moved to Ann Arbor in 1843, and in 1844, he was appointed assistant professor of chemistry at the University of Michigan. Then, in 1846, Douglas was made a full professor of chemistry. Dr. Douglas had charge of the erection of the observatory, the south wing of the main building, the Medical College and the waterworks. For a time, Dr. Douglas was dean of the medical faculty, and he introduced the laboratory method of instruction, then nearly unknown in such institutions.

Right: Silas H. Douglas. *Courtesy of the Bentley Historical Library, Michigan University Library, Faculty Portrait File, Box 1.*

Below: Dr. Douglas's house on the south side of Huron Street, between Division and State Streets. *Courtesy of the Bentley Historical Library, Douglas Family Collection, Box 9.*

"In 1858 the chemical laboratory was built according to his plans and he was put at its head, making it, in the words of Dr. Tappan, 'one of the most complete and efficient in our country.' To the development of this laboratory he devoted the best years of his life," noted Samuel Beakes in *Past and Present of Washtenaw County, Michigan*.

Dr. Douglas was active in the city of Ann Arbor, organizing the Ann Arbor Gas Company in 1869. He was elected mayor of the city in 1871 and again in 1872. During his time as mayor, he reorganized the police force and introduced a city license system of the liquor trade.

Since Dr. Douglas oversaw the construction of the Chemistry Building and had general charge and supervision of the department, he in time became director of the laboratory. While at this time, other departments of the university were sustained by university funds or legislative appropriations, the Chemistry Department was to a great degree self-sustaining.

The means by which the department was made self-sustaining were, according to *Regents v. Rose*, Douglas:

> *A stock of chemicals and apparatus adequate to the wants of the department was always kept on hand for the use and consumption of laboratory students. These were purchased from eastern dealers in considerable quantities, and, therefore at wholesale prices; they were sold to the students at the retail or catalogue prices of these dealers. The profits, which were considerable, beyond what was required for renewal of the stock were, under the direction of the Regents, applied in part to the payment of salaries of assistants, and in part to successive laboratory enlargements.*

Someone had to stay in the laboratory during business hours to oversee the stock of chemicals and the use of the apparatus and to dispense items to students as needed. In addition to these duties, someone had to keep the accounts and collect the fees when due. Dr. Douglas, because of his other duties, could not have done this. For this reason, these duties were performed by an assistant in the laboratory, who, like Douglas, was appointed by the regents. This assistant in the laboratory in time became known as the accountant of the laboratory.

Dr. Preston B. Rose was the assistant in the laboratory, or the accountant, from April 1866. Dr. Rose graduated from the University of Michigan in 1861 and enlisted in the Fifth Michigan Infantry Regiment on March 31,

The Chemistry Building designed by Dr. Douglas, where students studied and a few may have cheated the university. *Courtesy of the Bentley Historical Library.*

1863. He was wounded in action, resulting in the loss of a leg, and was honorably discharged on October 27, 1864.

Before Rose was appointed accountant, the laboratory had been a small affair and was not enlarged until the summer of 1866. Until then, the system of accounting was imperfectly carried out. Dr. Douglas was aware of the problems, and in his report to the regents in 1865, he stated that the laboratory needed a competent accountant. He urged the regents to appoint an assistant, with a salary adequate to secure one. The regents responded by appointing Dr. Rose as an assistant professor and charged him with the duty of accountant at a salary of $500. The old system of accounts remained in use until June so Rose could become familiar with it. Rose soon suggested certain improvements, which were approved by Dr. Douglas and put into effect.

Under this new system, when a student applied for admission to the laboratory, the student had to make a deposit of ten dollars, paid to Dr. Rose in his role as assistant. Dr. Rose then gave the student a receipt from a book of blank vouchers with accompanying stubs. On the receipt was the number of the receipt, the date, the name of the student and the amount deposited. On the back of the receipt was printed a blank certificate intended to be filled with the amount paid at the final settlement and signed by the student. The receipts, called tickets, entitled students to a table at the laboratory when a vacancy occurred in the ordered issued.

When a student did not enter the laboratory course for any reason, then upon return of the receipt, the deposit would be refunded by the assistant. Then, the receipt would be turned over to the director, Dr. Douglas, and by him destroyed. The stub in the book would be marked cancelled by a diagonal line drawn across it. Should a student enter the course, then at some time the account would be settled, and the student would turn over the receipt. Sometimes, when a student failed to return his receipt, a duplicate was made and the account would be closed.

On the first of each month of the school year, or soon after, Douglas and Rose would look over the accounts. Money paid to Rose would be turned over to Douglas, and Douglas would turn the money over to the regents of the university. Dr. Douglas would report to the regents each June on the money received at the laboratory.

Dr. Preston B. Rose. *Courtesy of the Bentley Historical Library, Michigan University Library, Faculty Portrait File, Box 4.*

Then, at the October 1975 meeting of the regents, a resolution was unanimously adopted requiring the director of the laboratory to render quarterly accounts of all money received for the sale of chemicals to the students. The director was further to present duplicate vouchers, "as in all other departments, covering all payments, in accordance with the existing law."

That same month, Dr. Douglas informed University of Michigan president James Burrill Angell that he had discovered a deficit in the account of the laboratory. President Angell, with Dr. Douglas and Dr. Prescott, examined the records for the year 1874–75 and found the deficit to be $831.10. When confronted with the findings of this examination, Dr. Rose paid a portion of the amount. In November 1875, Dr. Rose paid the remaining $645, having raised the money by placing a mortgage on his house.

Further investigation revealed discrepancies in the accounts of the laboratory for previous years. President Angell informed the executive committee of the board of regents of what had been discovered. Regents Walker and McGowan of the committee at once visited Ann Arbor and called on Dr. Rose. They told Dr. Rose that further examination of the

James Burrill Angell, president of the University of Michigan. *Courtesy of the Bentley Historical Library.*

accounts had revealed deficiencies for the preceding years. They asked Dr. Rose to secure the university against further loss. He turned over to the treasurer of the university a trust deed to his house.

To determine the amount of the missing money, a new committee was appointed consisting of Regents Gilbert, E.C. Walker and McGowan. The committee reported on December 21, 1875, that it had examined the accounts of the laboratory for several years and found a deficit of $4,718.62. In the judgment of the committee, most—if not all—of the deficit was in the hands of Dr. Rose. The committee further reported that Dr. Rose had rendered it every needed assistance until the fact of the deficit had been made public. From that time on, Dr. Rose had declined to render the committee further aid and had absented himself from the meetings.

Immediately after the presentation of the report to the regents, Dr. Rose appeared before the board and read a statement. In his statement, Dr. Rose described the methods of keeping accounts in the laboratory used by him and Dr. Douglas. He asserted his innocence of intentional wrongdoing and demanded that the director, Dr. Douglas, and himself "be brought face to face before some court or disinterested body of intelligent and competent men, and then and there be required to produce their proofs, and submit such questions to the opinions and judgment of such court."

The board of regents then voted to suspend Dr. Rose from his duties until further action of the board. Then the board voted to appoint a committee to investigate thoroughly the accounts of Dr. Douglas. This committee reported in June 1876 that it had found $4,332.65 to be in the hands of Dr. Rose and $1,174.65 in the hands of Dr. Douglas. To this, Dr. Douglas claimed that certain red lines and initials purporting to be his on receipts for money received by him from Dr. Rose were forgeries.

Shirley W. Smith, in *James Burrill Angell*, published in 1954, wrote:

> *The year 1876 was an election year, and the virus known as "politics" injected itself and spread, resulting in due course in there coming upon the Board two by election and one by appointment to a vacancy, three new Regents, pledged to themselves at least, to "see justice done." But secular politics, it turned out, could learn something of bitterness and hatred from the Methodists on the one hand who espoused the cause of Dr. Rose, "the underdog," and on the other hand from the other sects who were for Dr.*

> *Douglas, or at least against the Methodists. The chief anti-Douglas, pro-Rose spokesman soon became Mr. Rice Beal, publisher and editor of the Ann Arbor* Courier *always an ardent Methodist, a power in local and state Republican politics, and a man of great force and viselike pertinacity.*

In January 1877, the Michigan state legislature, urged on by a 10-page printed statement by Beal on the unfairness of the proceedings of the president and board against Rose, appointed a joint committee to "make a thorough and exhaustive investigation." After two months of testimony, which filled a 740-page book, the committee made its report. The committee placed the amount of the defalcation at $5,827.82, of which $497.30 was charged to Dr. Rose and $4,477.47 to Dr. Douglas. That same month, Dr. Douglas was dismissed from the faculty.

The case went to trial on July 5, 1877, and after five weeks, Rose was found liable for $4,624.40 and Douglas for the remainder. The court allowed Dr. Douglas credit for interest on money advanced for the laboratory, for traveling expenses and so forth. The controversy was still far from over.

"Two new Regents took their seats on the Board in January 1878," wrote Howard H. Peckham in *The Making of the University of Michigan.*

> *They and two others were "Rosemen," calling themselves the "People's Regents." The other four favored Douglas. Neither side could carry a motion, and debate was long and bitter. Former Regent McGowan, now a representative in Congress, wrote to Angell from Washington and advised him to leave the University if another offer came to him. "It's a glorious day for fools and demagogues," he added.*

"These four, the self-styled 'People's Regents,'" wrote Smith in his biography of Angell,

> *on occasions when less than the entire Board membership was present, were at times only prevented from taking action by the precipitate withdrawal of opponents, resulting in loss of a quorum. At the meeting of March 26 and 27, 1878, with only the four "People's Regents" present, though three other Regents had been present and had withdrawn but to remain in the near vicinity of the meeting place, there were recorded no less than eighteen*

Students at work in the Chemistry Laboratory. *Courtesy of the Bentley Historical Library.*

> *separate adjournments after the President wearily announced "no quorum." A number of these intervals of adjournment were for ten minutes only.*

"A new factor helped resolve the situation," wrote Peckham in *The Making of the University of Michigan.*

> *Joseph B. Steere, '68, '70, with a consuming interest in natural science, started on a leisurely trip around the world in 1870 with financial backing from Beal. He intended to send back to the University any interesting specimens he found, and in 1872 did send from South America an immense number of butterflies, bird skins, tropical woods, insects, fish, shells, fossils, and rocks. He also contributed regular travel letters to Beal's newspaper. His journey continued to the East Indies and China. By 1874 the quantity of specimens exceeded 15,000 items. Thousands more were received at the University in 1875. At Singapore Steere received a cable that he was granted an honorary PhD, the first ever given by Michigan. On his return in 1876, he was appointed assistant professor of paleontology.*

"As Beal was surety for Rose's immense debt," continued Peckham,

> *he would not be quiet. In June 1878 he was able to persuade the Regents to buy a half interest in the Beal-Steere collection for the University Museum at the price of their claim against Rose. The other half interest was a gift. Still, Rose partisans were not satisfied. At a February 1879 meeting of the Regents with the legislature's joint committee on the University, from which two pro-Douglas Regents were absent, a resolution was passed that upon request of the joint committee the Board would appoint Rose assistant professor of chemistry again. It was adopted by a vote of four to two. The decision was greeted locally by a bonfire, cannon firing, and a parade led by a band to Rose's house. Rose taught only two more years and retired.*

Douglas had not been satisfied with the decision of the court, which charged him with $1,047.47. The court ruled that the university owed Douglas credit for expenses on behalf of the laboratory, traveling expenses and other items. This sum was almost equal to his debt to the university. The university, by this ruling, owed Douglas $17.46.

No, Douglas was not satisfied with the ruling, and he carried the case on to the Michigan State Supreme Court. The regents chose not to employ counsel in the appeal in order to save the university the expense. The court rendered its decree in January 1881 in favor of Dr. Douglas. The university paid Douglas $2,045.80 plus costs, at $1,605.94, for a total of $3,651.74.

The ruling of the court brought the Douglas-Rose controversy to an end. "However," wrote Lewis G. Vander Velde,

> *severe as was the financial cost of the controversy, of far greater significance was the loss in prestige resulting from the bitter factional quarrels within the board of Regents, the sharp hostility toward the University engendered among members of the state legislature, the violent abuse indulged in by many of the newspapers of the state, the countless charges of bad faith and double-dealing, the sectarian animosities aroused between Methodists and non-Methodists, and the vindictiveness stirred up among groups in the faculty.*

Still, the bad feelings stirred up by the controversy could still be felt in Ann Arbor as late as the 1940s.

4

Death of a Student

On the evening of Tuesday, November 11, 1890, there was a rush of university students at the Ann Arbor Post Office. The result was that some of the students ended up spending the night in the city jail. The arrest and incarceration of the students caused bitter feelings toward the local authorities among the students. The next day, a rumor spread about the campus that there would be another rush on the post office that evening. Consequently, when the evening mail arrived at the post office that evening, there were hundreds of students in the vicinity. The crowd was orderly, as it was understood that should an officer interfere with the students, that officer would be rushed. No officer interfered with the students, and the evening seemed to be passing peacefully—until 9:30 p.m., when gunshots were heard.

The gunshots were fired, not in anger, but in celebration. That same day was the wedding of George Stoll, a member of Company A of the local militia, and Mary E. Thurston. Some members of Company A decided to give the newly married couple a charivari.

To prepare for the charivari, Quartermaster Sergeant Sheldon Granger had asked Ann Arbor mayor Charles Manly for permission to fire five volleys at the house. Mayor Manly later said he had refused to grant permission. Sergeant Granger then asked if the company could go in a body to the house. Mayor Manly said that over this he had no control. The mayor's story was corroborated by witnesses.

The courthouse at Ann Arbor was built in the 1870s and was the setting for many notable trials. The building was demolished in the 1950s. *Courtesy of the Bentley Historical Library.*

That evening, ten or twelve members of the company, along with a number of young men who were not members, removed weapons from the armory. Now armed with muskets, they marched with the drum corps of the Sons of Veterans to the couple's house on South Division Street, between Jefferson and William Streets. When the men were assembled in front of the house, they fired several volleys of blank cartridges. Once the men were finished firing the volleys, they were invited in for supper, and they entered the house.

The students, thinking the shots were a continuation of the trouble from the night before, hurried from all directions to see what was going on. Quickly, a steady stream of students poured into the street, some giving the college yell. Within five minutes of the first volley, some one thousand students had gathered on the street. When the students found out that it was a wedding, they could have left the scene but instead remained, jeering and giving the university yell. Someone from the yard said, "This is the biggest crowd of ignorant people I ever saw!"

A bird's-eye view of Ann Arbor, 1890. *Courtesy of the Bentley Historical Library.*

After about half an hour, the members of the company decided to leave, as something had to be done to get the students to go away. Capitan Anderson, commander of the company, was a guest at the wedding with his wife. He reasoned that if the members of the company left the house, the students would go as well. The members of the company, and those who had come with them, were ready to leave and take on the students in a fight. Capitan Anderson told the men to go but to leave the guns at the house. As Capitan Anderson later said, "I told the boys when they were in the house, and when they decided to go out and fight, that they must leave their guns there and fight with their fists if they must fight. I only allowed them to take their guns away on a promise to return to the armory."

The members of the company, and those who had come with them, formed in a single file on the street in front of the house. Then, the company began to march down Division Street toward Liberty Street, under the command of Quartermaster Sergeant Granger. As the company marched away from the house, the students began to follow, yelling and jeering as they did, in an irregular but compact mass. A few of the students called out "Rush!" but no such action was taken. The members of the company would later claim that the students threw mud at them and struck the men at the rear of the line with their canes.

Ford Belford, a student at the university, was in his room on South University, along with his roommate, Irving James Dennison, when they

Irving Dennison, the student killed in the mêlée with local militia. *Courtesy of Bill Stewart.*

heard the volley fired. Belford and Dennison went to see what was going on and then began to return home by way of Williams Street. The two met some other students and started back toward Division Street. Belford and Dennison saw the company march past.

"Quite a crowd followed them," recalled Belford later.

> *The militia started down on the east side, and at Williams Street crossed to the west side. We then went on the east side. The militia had turned down Liberty Street by the time we were at Williams Street. We kept on the east side of Division Street to Library, when we stopped. A crowd was there and the militia had stopped. Pretty soon from where we were standing we could see the militia form in a straight line across Library Street, at or a little below the red church. The crowd began to stretch across the street east of where the militia was stationed.*

The noise made by the students had been so great that Quartermaster Sergeant Granger was having trouble making himself heard. The members of the company had not heard some of his orders. He had no trouble making himself understood to someone in the crowd who was jeering him when he shouted, "If you don't keep still over there, I'll break your neck!"

Granger tried to say something else but was not heard, as the crowd gave the university yell. At this, Granger drew his sword and, waving it, called, "Knock hell out of them boys!"

What happened next was perhaps one of the worst hand-to-hand fights ever witnessed in the city of Ann Arbor. The militiamen were without bayonets but used the butt ends of their guns as clubs to good advantage. The students were armed with fence posts and stones. The fight may have lasted about ten minutes. Everyone who played a major role in the mêlée was hurt in some way.

As the company rushed forward, Granger was struck in the forehead with a brick thrown by someone in the crowd. He fell to the ground and was carried off. The blow caused a fracture to his skull, and a piece of his skull was later removed. For a time, it was feared that he would die, but Granger pulled through and recovered.

"The militia did not keep together but scattered out and used the butt end of their muskets as clubs," recalled Belford.

> *We were standing together when they started towards the crowd, and we retired a little towards States Street. One man, with his musket, started at me and I moved backward and he stopped. I again turned around and as I did so I saw a man with his musket, using it as a club, hit Mr. Dennison with the butt end of it on the forehead. I was ten or fifteen feet away at the time. I could not recognize who it was. Mr. Dennison seemed dazed and was likely to fall, and I went and took hold of him. Mr. Houck, a senior medic, came to my assistance, and we took Mr. Dennison to Dr. Vaughn's house on State Street, and as the doctor wasn't home, we took him to the University hospital.*

The company re-formed and made a second charge on the students. Once this was over, the company turned and marched to the armory. The students turned and returned to the campus. Several others had been hurt in the fight, but none seriously.

At the hospital, Dennison was worked on by the doctors but lost consciousness at midnight. He died at eight minutes after five o'clock in the morning. He was an only son who had come to Ann Arbor to enter the Literary Department in the freshman class that year. His parents arrived from their home in Toledo that morning, but after he had died.

"Mrs. Dennison, his mother, broke completely down and had to be carried into the room where her dead boy was placed: as for the father, he was rendered speechless, the great pain he was suffering showing itself but too plainly upon his countenance," reported the *Detroit Evening News* of Thursday, November 13, 1890.

"Dr. C.B. Nancrede," reported the *Ann Arbor Argus* of Friday, November 14, 1890,

> *who made the postmortem examination, found a cut reaching to the bone over the right eye parallel to the eye bone. There was a fracture involving the anterior and middle fossae of the skull. There were many lines of fracture dividing the bones forming these cavities into some twelve or more main fragments. One line of fracture passed through the opening in the skull on the right side which transmits one of the large blood vessels to the membranes of the brain, causing a giving away of that vessel. The limits of the clot resulting from this injury of this vessel, extended from the median line of the base of the skull upwards to within two inches of the median line above, measuring from before backwards five inches. The force of the blow received was sufficient to cause death.*

Ford Belford, the roommate of Dennison, later said:

> *I could see nothing done to cause the assault by the militia, except giving the University yell. I saw no stones thrown. We were behind the crowd when the assault was made. We were not there when the soldiers halted on Liberty Street. I heard no commands given as I was eighty or ninety feet away. When Mr. Dennison was struck, he was ten or fifteen feet from where we originally stood.*

"The largest crowd that was ever gathered in chapel collected this morning," reported the *Detroit Evening News* of Thursday, November 13, 1890.

> *After the usual services Dr. Angell started to make some remarks, but the grief he was suffering over the sad occurrence of last night forbid anything more than the simple statement that the sad case was in the hands of the authorities. The ladies of the literary department are doing a most gracious thing. Subscriptions are being collected by them for a handsome floral offering to accompany the remains of Dennison to his home. In all the rows that the students have ever had in this university, this is the first that has resulted fatally.*

That same day, the coroner, Martin Clark, empanelled a jury and, after viewing the body, adjourned until 2:00 p.m. that afternoon. When the inquest convened, the first witness called was Ford Belford, the roommate of Dennison. He was followed by Dr. Nancrede, who had made the postmortem examination. The last witness called that day was Paul Meyer, who said he saw Dennison struck.

"One man hit him across the arm with the butt of a gun," Meyer said, as reported by the *Ann Arbor Argus* of Friday, November 14, 1890.

> *Another solider stepped up and told him to go, and I think he said, "Why shall I go?" One of the soldiers said, "I'll show you why" and swung his gun around and hit him across the face. The soldier went across the road to the northwest corner after he struck him. I was about ten feet away. The man who struck Dennison was about five feet eight inches in height and stout. It was dark and I couldn't tell whether he had a beard or not.*

The inquest was then adjourned until the next day.

A Dr. Jackson, who lived near the site of the charge, told the inquest:

> *I saw the whole thing from my second story window, that is, that part of the affair which happened on Liberty Street. The company was marching down Liberty and at a point below the German church they halted. What was said I could not hear, but I distinctly saw a number of students stoop down, appear to pick up something and go through with the motions of throwing it. Whether they did or not I cannot say.*

The post office in Ann Arbor. Student rushes here caused the tension that led to the death of a student. *Courtesy of the Bentley Historical Library.*

On Friday, November 14, 1890, some fifteen hundred students of the university accompanied the remains of Dennison to the Michigan Central Railroad Depot, and a committee selected by his class traveled to Toledo to attend the funeral.

The class of 1894 had passed a resolution:

> *WHEREAS, God in his Divine Providence has seen fit to remove from our midst a beloved and respected classmate, Irving J. Dennison, and,*
>
> *WHEREAS, by his untimely death, in the midst of a bright and promising career, we, in common with the whole University of Michigan, have sustained a serious and much regretted loss, therefore,*
>
> Resolved, *That the class of '94, mourning the death of its member, extend to the bereaved parents their deep and heartfelt sympathy, trusting that the tender compassion of a merciful Father will console them in this hour of sorrow, and be it further*

> Resolved, *That an engrossed copy of these resolutions be sent to the parents of the deceased, and that copies be forwarded to the college papers.*

The inquest was continued over several more days but failed to find anyone who could name the killer of Dennison. Feelings toward Ann Arbor mayor Charles Manly began to grow hot, as some saw him as being morally responsible for the case.

"This morning the early risers in coming down State Street were greeted with the spectacle of Mayor Manly hung in effigy," reported the *Detroit Evening News* of the same day. "The mayor refuses to have it torn down and thinks it was done by friends of the students who were incarcerated in jail Tuesday night."

The students were becoming hotheaded and injudicious, according to the *Detroit Evening News* of Saturday, November 16, 1890. The paper reported that there was talk among the students of some night going over to the house of the mayor to "paint it red." Mayor Manly noted that his house was white and brown, the colors he wanted it, and he did not want the students to waste their time and energy changing the color. "The mayor is a man of great determination and is prepared for any such emergency," noted the *Detroit Evening News.*

In spite of the determination of the coroner and others, Dennison's killer was never found. No arrest was made, and the case faded from memory. The militia company was abolished because of the mêlée and a new one formed.

5

Jack the Hugger

From January 1900 until October 1903, the city of Ann Arbor lived in terror of a fiend called "Jack the Hugger." This man would approach young women on the street during the evening hours in what was called "a most startling manner."

"His first appearance was reported from S. Division St. about 10 days ago," reported the *Ypsilanti Commercial* of Thursday, January 11, 1900,

> *when a man slid up behind a lady as she was going along the sidewalk in the evening, threw his arms around her, kissed her and then ran away. The matter was not reported to the officers for a few days, when a very similar experience was reported from Jefferson St. The officers have been quietly watching a suspect since that time, but he seems to be the wrong party, for the hugger got in his work on Ingalls St. a few nights ago, at the very time that an officer was watching the man who was supposed to have done the other jobs. Still another case is reported of the same kind of work on Thayer St. last evening. In the other cases the women have been so badly scared that, as the man attacks them from behind, they have been unable to give any satisfactory description of their assailant. The lady last evening had a little more presence of mind, and is able to give quite an idea of the man, whom she describes as of medium size, with a black moustache. She thinks him to be about 40 years of age.*

Although the incidents may seem to have a humorous aspect to them, they were cause for concern. This was a man with serious metal or emotional issues that today would require treatment. A man sneaking up behind women, kissing them and then running away appears odd. The danger was that this behavior could, unless stopped, escalate into violence, perhaps even rape. Here was a man no father or brother would want his daughter or sister to encounter.

About a year later, a Miss Alice C. Manwaring, who lived with her parents at 516 Chubb Street, was returning home early in the evening of Monday, January 28, 1901, when, while walking on Spring Street, she noticed a man crossing the street in front of her. When the man reached her, he demanded her money. She told the man she had no money and tried to pass, but the man blocked her way. At this, reported the *Washtenaw Times* of Tuesday, January 29, 1901, "she screamed, but grabbed her assailant by the throat and pushed him aside." The man then said he would go home with her. For this "impudence," she gave his face a slap. He gave Miss Manwaring no further trouble, as her screams were attracting attention.

"Miss Manwaring thought that it might have been done for an alleged joke and said nothing to her parents about the matter until other ladies who witnessed the affair from their homes nearby," noted the *Washtenaw Times*, "being attracted by her screams, could not see the joke and notified the sheriff's office, and Deputy Sheriff Kelsey called at her home for particulars."

"If some smart aleck is doing that work over there," commented the *Washtenaw Times*, "it is time to call a halt. A good dose of lead or a term in prison would be about the right kind of joke on him."

The *Ann Arbor Courier-Register* of Wednesday, January 30, 1901, reprinted the account, adding that three other women on the north side had been approached in a like manner. Each escaped from her assailant and ran. None of the women had known of the others. The descriptions given by the women agreed, except some said he wore a black cap and others said he wore a gray cap. The three had come forward after reading the account in the *Washtenaw Times*.

"There are some indications," concluded the account, "that the miscreant who played 'Jack the Hugger' last fall, has broken out again in a new role."

A new appearance by Jack the Hugger was reported by the *Ann Arbor Daily Argus* of Monday, October 14, 1901. According to the account, a young woman was walking home at about 9:00 p.m. on North Division Street when a man siezed her by the arm. She wrenched herself free from the man and gave him a blow over the head with an umbrella. This enraged the man, who struck her with his clenched fist. "This staggered her for a moment," noted the account, "but she started and ran to her home, which was only a short distance away, and reached it in a nearly exhausted condition."

There were attempts to hunt down Jack the Hugger. Young women would go out in the evening hours, while muscular men waited in hiding. Then there were the young men who dressed as women to lure Jack the Hugger out into the open. At least one young woman walked with a handful of pepper to throw into his face, should he approach her. A great deal of time and effort was spent trying to bring him to justice—but to no avail, as he failed to fall into any of these traps.

Then, in October 1903, Jack the Hugger approached a woman in the sixth ward. This time, the woman recognized him as someone she knew. She threatened him with arrest and exposure. "He begged for mercy," reported the *Evening Times* of Saturday, October 3, 1903, "and in order to shield herself from notoriety which would follow a prosecution, she consented to desist from making out a warrant on the condition that he would sign a statement acknowledging his actions and promising never to repeat his insults to anyone."

He agreed, and the terror of Jack the Hugger came to an end.

6

Dime Novel Disappearance of Albert Patterson

Albert Patterson was a medical student at the University of Michigan who, in May 1903, was only a few weeks away from graduation and receiving his diploma and the right to practice medicine. He was at this time about thirty years of age, standing over six feet in height, with broad shoulders and merry blue eyes. A great future seemed to be laid out before him. He was rooming at the home of deputy postmaster George Vandawarker at 910 Huron Street East. Then, on the morning of Wednesday, May 27, 1903, he disappeared under circumstances that, as local newspapers phrased it, "would make a dime novelist turn green with envy."

On the morning of Wednesday, May 27, 1903, Vandawarker went out to mow his lawn. On his lawn, he found a white hat, such as Patterson wore, with a hole about one inch long. The hole appeared to have been made by some blunt instrument, with hair and what looked like blood around it. On the inside of the hat was the word "Patterson."

Patterson was not to be found in his room. "The bed in his room," reported the *Ann Arbor Daily Argus* of Thursday, May 24, 1903, "showed he had not gone to bed, although the bed clothing was turned back and a pillow moved as if he had started to go to bed."

The day before, Patterson had studied with his fiancée, Maude Hinman, also a medical student, until almost midnight. Maude Hinman was said to have been a young lady of modest mien, a pronounced brunette with a slight build and a general bearing of refinement and culture. She had a face, it was said, befitting a mind given to seriousness and gravity. The two had studied at her place of residence. It was Patterson's practice to write a letter or two each night before going to bed. He may have left the house to mail his letters.

Vandawarker informed the police, and a search of Patterson's room was made. In a desk drawer was found an envelope on which was written:

> *May 21—12.30*
> *Still alive.*
> *To be opened in case of my death or disappearance.*

Inside the envelope was a letter of explanation:

> *I will be the only one to ever read this so I suppose if it is a silly thing to do no one else will get to enjoy it.*
>
> *It's late and I suppose that has something to do with it, but I do feel nervous.*
>
> *When I was in San Antonio in the winter of '97 and '98 I met with an experience. I wandered into the Mexican part of town, it's too late to tell it all. Suffice to say I stumbled into a meeting of an organization. I was immediately caught, gagged and tied. They went through a lot of Tommy-rot but I could see that they were dead in earnest in it all. They made me swear to a lot of things. I thought it was a sort of lark. Then they led me out through a long tunnel blind-folded and took me across the river there. I was leary of ever going back there to look for the place and I never saw any of those present again. I came north, enlisted, went to war, was discharged and have been here in school ever since and have never heard anything. I had almost forgotten it until I got a note some time since warning me that I had forfeited my life and it would be taken.*
>
> *Rats! I'm ashamed to write this even for myself to read, but someway I can't shake myself free of a sort of dread.*
>
> *I got another note and then this last one which I all but threw away. It didn't seem possible that anything could come of it but—well something of the old dread of that night in Texas is on me and maybe this will free me of it. So if I am found dead or missing our old friend "Maximo" has fixed*

it. This dreaded thing has made me feel more nervous than I did before. Sounds so preposterous. Wonder how a thin knife feels in the back? Maybe Maximo wants me to cough up again. He is not a Mexican and so a worse fanatic than they are.

Well, peace to my ashes.

ALBERT A. PATTERSON

May 19, 1903

News of Patterson's disappearance proved to be a great strain on his fiancée, Maude Hinman, and she was reported to have been left completely prostrated and was confined to bed.

A senior medical student examined the stains on Patterson's hat and concluded that the stains were not blood but a red wood dye. Then, Dean Vaughan made a personal examination of the stains and found that some of the smaller stains were blood.

Maude G. Hinman, at the time she graduated from the University of Michigan. *Courtesy of the Bentley Historical Library, University of Michigan Photographs, Vertical File, UM Medical School Classes, 1903.*

"But," said Dean Vaughan, "nobody believes that Patterson has been murdered. The bloodstains may have come from a prick on the finger and smeared on the hat," reported the *Ann Arbor Courier-Register* of Wednesday, May 27, 1903.

By now, the public was treating the disappearance as something of a joke. The *Ann Arbor Daily Argus* received an unsigned letter, which was published by the paper on Friday, May 22, 1903. The letter read:

> *To the Editor—On the night of Mr. Patterson's murder, the writer of this saw a large object ascend the air, rising upward about five hundred feet and shoot off in a southerly direction. Since reading the terrible announcement of the death &, of Mr. Patterson, the writer is convinced that the large object which he saw was nothing else than a flying machine which carried off the remains of our young friend to Mexico to be dealt with as the enormity of his act toward the organization which he had betrayed, deserves. I would give my name to this information but that I fear the same dreadful doom would overtake me at the hands of those foul fiends, should they know who is giving them away.*
>
> *Yours in dread.*

On Wednesday, June 3, 1903, the *Evening Times* reported that a day or two after Patterson had disappeared, a wooden butter plate with a bullet hole through it was picked up on the bank of the Huron River. This was found near Truman Albor's house at the Whitmore Lake crossing, the report noted. Mr. Albor kept the plate in his possession until advised to turn it over to the sheriff, which he did. On the bottom of the wooden butter plate was a message, which read:

May 22, '03
Albert Patterson's headless
Body will be found by dragging
The river opposite here
Signed,
[Symbols of two crossed bowie knives and skull and crossbones.]

"As the river is so low now," reported the *Evening Times*, "owing to the recent bursting of the dam, there is no necessity of raking the river."

Soon after the *Evening Times* story, a man called "Tug" Wilson, an employee at Fred Besimer's saloon, told Marshal Keisey he had seen two students nail the plate to the tree. After the students left, he had gone up and read the message. He thought it a little joke and said nothing of it, until after the story was told in the papers.

No trace of Patterson had been found in Ann Arbor by the beginning of August, but by then, reports were coming in from those who believed they had seen him in other places. A young woman named Emma Beckwith of Greencastle, Indiana, claimed she had seen him in Montreal in July.

At about the same time Miss Beckwith said she saw Patterson in Montreal, another young woman from Greencastle, Indiana, arrived in Ann Arbor, settled his debts and removed his personal property from the city. The name she gave was not her own, and she gave no reason for her action. No one ever found out who she was or the reason for her interest in Patterson.

On Thursday, October 22, 1903, the *Evening Times* reported that Patterson had been found in Oklahoma. "Credence is given the report at the young man's home from the fact that his parents have ceased to prosecute the search which they began with much vigor, and while they refuse to say whether they know his whereabouts, it is apparent that they do know. It is positively asserted in Logansport that no further effort will be made to throw light on this mystery," noted the *Evening Times*. The reason given for Patterson's disappearance was that he was to marry two women on the same day.

The mystery of the disappearance came to an end later that month with the announcement of the marriage of Patterson to Maude Hinman at Saginaw. It was at Saginaw that Dr. Maude Hinman had opened her medical practice after her graduation from the University of Michigan. She and Patterson were married at her home at 415 North Webster Street, and here a reporter for the *Saginaw News* went to interview them. To the reporter, Patterson admitted that the reason for his disappearance was his engagement to two women at the same time. Patterson said he had no idea at the time about how he was to extricate himself from the difficulty.

"I'm frank to confess that I shouldn't have made my exit in quite as sensational a manner as I did," said Patterson.

> *The trouble with me is that I've got too vivid an imagination. My departure was due to one of those brain fancies which look perfectly plausible the*

> *night before and appear the height of idiocy the next day. The trouble with me was that I didn't sleep on it, but acted on the spur of the moment, without taking into consideration that a man can't be kidnapped and killed by brigands with pomp and ceremony and then be allowed to come quietly back to life afterwards.*

"All that Mafia and Maximo business," continued Patterson,

> *you will understand was simply the product of a versatile thin-pan working over time. There wasn't any Mafia and as to Maximo, I think I got the idea of his being so bloodthirsty a villain from a cigar I smoked once by that name down in Texas which was the worst ever. I've been in Colorado ever since until my coming to Saginaw to marry the girl I "died for." I might tell you about the great mining interests I have out there, but I guess I've perpetrated enough pipe tales for one while.*

The reporter asked Patterson if he planned to finish his studies at the University of Michigan.

"Well, I hardly think so," answered Patterson. "It might prove too stout a proposition to face, although of course I could: there is nothing to prevent me doing so."

The reporter then asked Patterson about the red ink he smeared on the hat.

Patterson told the reporter it was not ink on the hat. "It was real blood. I have a scar on my finger yet where I slashed myself to drop it on."

"Deal with me kindly," said Patterson in conclusion. "I'll confess that it was a prank wholly unworthy of anyone of mature mind, although," he added, "they say all's fair in love and war."

7

Riot at the Star Theatre

In 1908, Albert Reynolds was the proprietor of the Star Theatre at 118 East Washington Street in Ann Arbor. This was, as noted by Kent Sagendorph in *Michigan: The Story of the University*,

> *a small dingy, single-store space which had been remodeled with an eye to future use as a nickelodeon if the flickering films ever became practical. The stage was about fifteen feet wide, which allowed only acrobats, specialty dancers and comics to get much of a response from their audiences, mostly composed of students and Ann Arbor workmen. Singers worked well there, but the kind of entertainment provided at the Star wasn't on a very high musical plane. In those days a singer was judged in such houses on the volume of audience response resulting from her bellowing of a popular refrain. If the audience howled too, she was a success.*

When Reynolds looked out on the audience each evening, he must have hoped to see few—or, better yet, no—students from the university. By this time, Reynolds had earned the animosity of the men who attended the university. Previous to taking on the management of the Star, Reynolds had operated a billiard hall and cigar store near the campus. When some of the young men ran up bills at the store, Reynolds would send the bill to their fathers for payment. Those young men, including those who were not suppose to be addicted to cigarettes, were not pleased to learn that their bills had been paid by their fathers. This was most likely one of many acts by Reynolds that caused bad feelings.

University students at this time were noisy, high-spirited and aggressive, but in the spirit of fun. "He felt," noted Sagendorph, "that if he didn't play some pranks or make some noise he wasn't being a typical college student."

The style of dress popular among students of the time may also have offended Reynolds's sense of decency. After all, this was the time when turtleneck sweaters were all the fashion, as well as

> *huge, wide-shouldered coats that looked about four sizes too large loom*[ing] *above short, thick, narrow-cuffed trousers, the cuff rolled up above the ankle. There was displayed about five inches of the wildest socks insane designers could concoct: polka dots, plaids, checks, black-and-white whirls like candy canes, and even plain purple now and then. The socks could be heard coming down William Street before the wearer could be identified. Long dangling watch fobs of leather or black moiré adorned with gold footballs, gold skulls, brass "M" letters, or something equally subtle, made such a costume an assault upon the senses. But college students everywhere dressed like that in 1910.*

When the student went to the Star, he went to make noise. On the night of Saturday, March 14, 1908, some students went to see the show at the Star. One of them, said to have been named Kamm, of Kentucky, was ordered out of the theatre for whistling. As Kamm was walking past Reynolds, it was later said, Reynolds made some insulting remark to him. At this, it was alleged, Kamm slapped Reynolds across the face. Special Officer Jack Schlimmer, who was escorting Kamm out of the building, struck Kamm on the head with his club, cutting his head and causing Kamm to fall to the sidewalk.

This treatment of Kamm caused bad feelings among the students, and a raid on the theater was planned to occur on Monday night. George Spathelf, Reynolds's partner, received information that the theater was to be raided. This information seems to have come from those who kept roomers and may have heard the student boarders talk of their plans. Chief of Police Apfel had also heard rumors of trouble to come. A letter was sent to Reynolds, unsigned and postmarked March 16, 3:20 p.m. It said, "Dirty Pup, Fair Warning." The letter was turned over to Chief Apfel. He was also told of possible trouble by the mayor and the sheriff.

Chief Apfel recruited some fifteen special officers for the night. The Ann Arbor City Council was scheduled to meet that evening, and Chief Apfel, before going to the council meeting, had met several bunches of students at Fourth and Washington Streets. He asked the students to disperse and then went to attend the council meeting.

At an early hour of the evening on Monday, March 16, 1908, Washington Street, from Main to Fourth, was filled with students. The students sang, "We're here because we're here, because we're here." As the evening

The Star Theatre, where students rioted. *Ann Arbor District Library website.*

progressed, more students arrived, and gangs passed along the street with the call: "Out for the Star Theatre." These were students mixed with town boys who had come to join the fun.

Trouble began when two students in the theater were arrested for stamping their feet and whistling. The two students were hustled out of the theater, and the crowd, which may have numbered some fifteen hundred, followed the officers and students to the jail. Near the jail, the crowd rushed the officers and pulled one of the students away from the officers. Then the crowd ran back to the theater, where, once it had gathered out front, someone threw a brick through the front window. This was the signal to begin an assault on the building. Now the crowd began to throw bricks and stones and other objects at the building. The star-shaped electric sign was a bull's-eye for the students armed with bricks and stones. Soon, the front of the building was wrecked.

Bricks and stones smashed the windows of the apartment next to the theater, where Fred Cook and his wife and four children lived. Fred's wife went into hysterics, and a doctor had to be called. The doctor stayed with Mrs. Cook for several hours. The front windows of Hoppe's Saloon next door were broken by hurled stones.

Then the students and town boys made a rush on the building and smashed in the front of the theater. As the assault began, the theater orchestra was playing "Sweethearts May Come and Sweethearts May Go" for the movie *Way Down East.* The orchestra gave a grand pause and, as it came to realize what was happening, the violin, drum and piano players made a quick run out the back door. The piano player, a Miss Rogers, lost twenty-five dollars worth of music, which was destroyed in the riot.

During the riot, the electric piano was carried out to the street where it was demolished. The movie projector was carried off as well, as were the receipts for the day, for some forty-five dollars, and the cash box.

Officer Zenas Sweet was on duty in the theater when the assault began. He did not see any students throw bricks at the building but did see sticks and stones thrown into the theater from outside. Officer Sweet heard threats made against Reynolds.

Officer Sweet left by the rear door with Albert Reynolds and his wife. Then, Officer Sweet returned to the theater. He saw the mechanical piano being pulled out of the theater and onto the street. Once the piano had been pulled out onto the street, a student played a few notes, and then it was ripped apart and pieces carried off as keepsakes.

Another who returned to the theater was Albert Reynolds, who at one time took hold of a double-barrel shotgun and threatened to go out and empty it into the crowd. The police took the gun from Reynolds. Reynolds remained in the theater until a late hour, much of that time in the basement of the building.

"One student climbed up on top of the building and tied a rope on the electric sign to rip it off. Three policemen went after him, but he climbed through the window and got away," reported the *Detroit Free Press* of Tuesday, March 17, 1908.

Summoned to the scene from the council meeting, Chief Apfel called on the crowd to disperse. At this point, Chief Apfel was hit with a rock. The police then began to make arrests. When a man was arrested by police, Chief Apfel heard cries of "Rush him! Kill him!"

"In making an arrest Chief Apfel dropped his hat," reported the *Detroit Free Press* of Tuesday, March 17, 1908. "As he stooped to recover it, a collegian hit the policeman and another kicked him as he rolled around on the walk."

The police tried to restore order but were unable to subdue the crowd. Officers would rush into the crowd and arrest a student, then carry him off to jail. Some students would follow but soon would see they were unable to rescue their fellow student.

At about 9:00 p.m., the police called the fire department to the scene to use its hose on the crowd. The firefighters coupled their hose to a hydrant and then turned to face the crowd. The crowd had scattered, and there were only small groups of three or four to be seen. Suddenly, a group of students rushed the hydrant to which the hose had been coupled. The firefighters tried to protect their equipment, but the students brushed them aside. Some three hundred feet of hose was cut. The students disconnected the hose from the hydrant and carried it one hundred feet away.

No further attempt was made by the firefighters to control the crowd; Sid Millard, chairman of the board of commissioners, ordered them back to the station. Millard said no one had a right to use the fire department for such a purpose.

Mayor Henderson was called from the meeting of the council as well. He tried to speak to the crowd but was unable to make himself heard. Mayor

Henderson returned to the council meeting at about 9:30 p.m. and reported on the state of affairs. A suggestion was made to call out the local military company. To this, Mayor Henderson explained that he had consulted with Captain Wilson, who told Mayor Henderson that the company could not be called out, except on order of the governor.

The council unanimously passed a resolution:

> *Resolved, That it is the consensus of opinion of this council that the persons arrested and in any way connected with the riot now on in this city should be prosecuted to the full extent of the law and on conviction given the maximum sentence.*

At about 10:00 p.m., University of Michigan president James B. Angell arrived on the scene. Suddenly, one hundred voices began to shout, "Hats! Hat! President Angell! President Angell!" The students removed their hats and stepped aside to let President Angell pass. Walking with him was Harry

President Angell later in life. *Courtesy of the Bentley Historical Library.*

Hutchins, the dean of the Law School. Standing in the entrance of the Star Theatre, President Angell addressed the crowd.

"Gentlemen," said President Angell, "this is deplorable! We wish you to follow Dean Hutchins and me home and go to bed! If any injustice has been done you, we will help you. In the morning we will do all in our power to assist you in getting the gentlemen out of jail. We or you can do nothing tonight."

President Angell and Dean Hutchins then walked to the campus, respectfully followed by a large number of the students. At the corner of Fourth and Washington Streets, President Angell said to a Mr. Dwyer that it was no use to appeal to the students.

"About half past ten, President Angell and Dean Hutchins drove down and again were spectators of what was now mostly a singing crowd of students who refused to go home. No public appeal was made at this time," reported the *Michigan Daily* on Tuesday, March 17, 1908.

The riot came to an end at about 11:30 p.m., after a bugle call was heard. "The bugler," reported the *Ann Arbor Daily Times* of Tuesday, March 17, 1908, "blew assembly in the armory, and the members of CIMNG gathered from all directions shortly before midnight. Intimidated by the sound of the call to arms for the militia, the students dispersed."

In all, eighteen students spent the night in jail. According to the *Michigan Daily* of Wednesday, March 18, 1908:

> *No place to sleep and hardly to sit down, dirty companions and filthy surroundings—such were the conditions under which the students arrested during the riot at the Star Theatre spent the night. They were locked in the main cell of the jail, in which fourteen tramps were also confined These tramps were more than dirty, and contributed materially to the discomforts of the place. One of them had some malignant skin disease, but was left lying in the cell with the other prisoners all evening. In all, thirty-two persons were crowded into one small room. There were no beds, all the furniture consisting of two tables and a few benches. The students were forced to take turns resting on these, and in this way given a chance to try to sleep for part of the night. The whole cell was indescribably filthy; dirt was piled up in the corners, and vermin were everywhere. No one was allowed to communicate with his friends or obtain legal advice during the morning.*

About noon some black coffee, molasses, and half a loaf of bread were given to the prisoners. This was the first food given them.

On the morning of Tuesday, March 17, 1908, Chief Apfel swore out fifteen complaints on the charge of rioting before Justice of the Peace Doty. To this, there was no minimum penalty, but the maximum penalty was not less than a year in the county jail or five years in the prison and a fine of $1,000. Dear Reed told the *Ann Arbor News-Argus* of that day: "By action of the board of regents any student serving a jail sentence must be expelled from college and it means dismissal for all who are guilty."

Word that the students were to be arraigned at 2:00 p.m. that afternoon quickly spread across the campus. By 1:00 p.m., one hundred students stood outside the door to the basement room in the courthouse, where Justice Doty had his court. When the doors to the courtroom were opened, the crowd surged into the small room, filling the benches and overcrowding the jury box. Some even perched on the judge's stand.

"Students stood on benches and soon the furniture commenced to crack and seats were broken. The crowd surged in on the windows and a pane of glass was cracked," noted the *Ann Arbor News-Argus* of Wednesday, March 18, 1908.

"It was like a turbulent sea and even the prosecutor could hardly get elbow room," continued the account. The accused were brought into the courtroom four at a time, each handcuffed to an officer. Bond was set at $1,000 for each. By afternoon, each of the fifteen had been released. They were scheduled to face examination on the charge on Friday morning, March 20, 1908.

This left three students who had been charged with disorderly conduct. They had been arrested near the jail, where they were on their way to provide bail for a friend. As one explained to the *Michigan Daily* of Wednesday, March 18, 1908: "We were called up about 1 o'clock by a friend who had been arrested, and we were turning the corner toward the jail when we met the officers. We explained our mission and asked what we could do. They grabbed us by our arms and said, 'We'll show you what you can do.' With that they hauled us into the jail, unlocked the turnstile and shoved us into this small hole." They went before Justice Doty that afternoon and were charged under the city ordinance with disorderly conduct and discharged after paying a fine of $4.65 each.

"All day long the Star Theatre was the object of general interest," reported the *Michigan Daily* on Wednesday, March 18, 1908. "Manager Reynolds has rushed workmen to the place and behind a screen of canvas they had been putting the show place in order. In daylight the damage to the place does not appear as badly as it did in the uncertain light of Monday night. The front can be quickly repaired. The interior was scarcely molested and a good sweeping will make the room ready for occupancy."

Reynolds told the *Michigan Daily*, "I am not catering to the trade of the students. Certainly we will open up again. We were ready to give a show this afternoon. Oh, we have a machine here; we have a supply of those things on hand, you know. I don't expect justice, but I am going to open up again, perhaps tomorrow."

That night, two more students were arrested, but not for having taken part in the riot. The two were leaving the Cook House when they ran into Officer Blackburn, who found that one had hidden a nickel-plated cuspidor under his coat. He arrested the pair and took them to the jail. The next day, the two were charged with larceny by Officer Blackburn, as Mr. Wheeler, proprietor of the Cook House, chose not to make a complaint against them. "These fellows were evidently a little intoxicated and did not know what they were doing," said Wheeler. Besides, he pointed out, the cuspidor was returned, so everything was all right. The two students were fined $10.00, plus $5.30 each.

The same night the two were arrested, the student body held a meeting at which it was decided to collect money from each class to cover the cost of damage to the Star Theatre.

"One of the boys who had been 'pinched,' C.H. Leete, a freshman law, who had taken time to investigate the exact damages after he was released from jail yesterday on bail, said that the damage to the store property amounted to about $125, Hoppe's window $19.50. Bert Reynolds' damage $900, pianist's music $25, and the 'mental anguish' to the people who occupied the rooms above the Star, $50, making a total of about $1,200. Adding the cost of attorney's fees the 'little fun' will cost easily in the neighborhood of $2,000," reported the *Ann Arbor Daily Times* of Wednesday, March 18, 1908.

The examination of the fifteen students accused of rioting began on the morning of Friday, March 20, 1908, in the basement courtroom of Justice

Doty. Police officers stood guard at the doors and made sure no more people were admitted into the room than the room could hold. An attorney named Cavanaugh read a petition addressed to Justice Doty and Andrew J. Sawyer. The petition read:

> *Gentlemen:—We, the undersigned business men of Ann Arbor, believing that the interests of our city and the great university, will be better served by avoiding any and all friction between them, and considering our interests mutual, and each dependent to a considerable degree upon the other, and desiring to prevent unnecessary publicity of the occurrence that we all deeply deplore, and knowing that the prosecution of these cases will result in no benefit to the city and burden the county with hundreds of dollars in costs, do hereby recommend that those arrested for the disturbance of March 16, last be discharged upon payment of all damage to property and all costs incurred to the city and county.*

The petition was signed by seventy-four citizens and businessmen of Ann Arbor, including Mr. Rinsey, the owner of the building damaged.

Prosecuting Attorney Sawyer intimated that some of those who signed the petition did so out of fear of being boycotted by the student population. City Attorney Dwyer suggested that the defendants waive examination and be bound over for trial in the circuit court.

On Monday, March 23, 1908, the *Ann Arbor Daily Times* reported:

> *Justice Doty said the signers of the petition evidently attributed to him a position he did not occupy; his function was to determine if there was probable cause to hold the defendants for circuit court and the petition should have been presented to the latter. H had no jurisdiction beyond this and the examination must proceed.*

The examination began against one of the students named Emerick. The prosecution called as witnesses University of Michigan President James Angell, Mayor Henderson, Chief Apfel and others. Although the case was made against only one of the students, all the students accused, with their lawyers, had to be in the courtroom the whole time. The examination that started on Friday was adjourned over the weekend and continued on

Monday. On Wednesday, March 25, 1908, Emerick was bound over to the circuit court for trial during the May term. The court then began the examination against a student named Rook.

The next day, Thursday, March 26, 1908, the *Ann Arbor News-Argus* published a letter from Mayor Henderson to Prosecuting Attorney Sawyer:

> *My Dear Sir:—In view of certain representations which have been made to me by responsible people in whom I have the utmost confidence, I desire to offer for your consideration a suggestion as to the very regrettable affair which has resulted in the examination now in progress before Justice Doty.*
>
> *You have already presented such an array of evidence as to the probable connection of one of the young men under arrest charged with riot as has led to his being bound over to the circuit court for trial, and others probably will likewise be bound over. Your determination in this matter is therefore fully recognized, the law has in a measure been vindicated and I believe the punishment the young men have already suffered will serve as a deterrent to a similar occurrence.*
>
> *I am informed that the students responsible for the riotous disturbance and destruction of property are ready to make good all property damage and apologize for their outrageous conduct. The prominent faculty members making these representations have the best interest of the university and the city at heart as well as ourselves, and their representations are therefore, I feel, entitled to weight. I share with them in the belief that the unpleasant notoriety our city and university are getting is extremely harmful to both. From all over the country I am from day to day receiving newspaper clippings which are most obnoxious and humiliating to me. In view of all these facts, do you not think the ends of justice might be substantially conserved, and the city and university safe guarded, at the same time by an adjournment of the present hearing for a week or two to ascertain whether or not it is possible to adjust this lamentable affair without a further long drawn out examination and a consequent possible delay of trial from term to term in the circuit court. I shall be pleased to have you give this matter such careful consideration as you may think it deserves and shall gladly acquiesce in such cause of action as you may finally determine upon.*

On Thursday, March 26, 1908, Rook was bound over for trial in the May term of the circuit court. Then the court took up the case of a student named Saul H. Meister of Detroit, whose case was bound over for trial in the circuit court on Friday, March 27, 1908. At this time, the remaining twelve students waved examination and were bound over for trial in the May term.

"This happy termination of the proceedings will enable the students to resume their school work and allay the excitement which the trial was occasioning in the community. The intervening weeks may now be devoted to reason, and it is more than probable that in that time the method may be found for bringing the whole subject to such a termination as will be honorable to all interests," noted the *Ann Arbor Daily Times* of Friday, March 27, 1908.

Although the cases of the students were now set for the May term of the circuit court, no one stood trial for the riot. Instead, the students of the university raised the money to pay for the damages to the building, and the charges were dropped. For those who had taken part in the riot, the events of that evening were either a source of shame or a pleasant memory. "The events of the evening are still treasured in memory by some," noted Shirley W. Smith in his biography, *Harry Burns Hutchins*, published in 1951. "Witness a substantial, but now wholly useless, part of the theater piano lovely cherished in his home by a dignified and distinguished Los Angeles Attorney!"

8

Mystery Surrounds Death of Foster Campbell

When a young son is late for supper, a mother is, of course, filled with concern. Hattie Campbell was worried on the evening of Thursday, January 19, 1911, as her nine-year-old son Foster was late for dinner. At about 5:00 p.m., she stepped outside the house at 823 West Washington Street in Ann Arbor and called for him in a loud voice. Her calls were heard by the neighbor, Mrs. Herron.

An hour before, Foster had been playing with Mrs. Herron's son, Louis, who was fourteen years of age; they had been making a toboggan. After school, the two had taken some tin from a shack, where they often played, for use on the toboggan. They planned to use the toboggan on a slide near the house. Foster picked up an axe and started back for the shack to knock off some more boards for use on the toboggan.

"Don't do that," said the Herron boy. "Maybe we won't want them."

Foster continued on toward the shack. The younger sister of the Herron boy wanted to go with Foster, but their mother told the her stay at the house. Soon after, she called her son inside and went to meet his older sister, Lucy, who was employed at the Varsity Laundry.

When Louis came back, he stayed in the house until a playmate came and asked him to go coasting on the Seventh Street hill, where almost all the children were playing. Just after Louis left for the hill, Mrs. Herron, who had returned from meeting Lucy, heard screaming from the direction of the

Campbell home. She paid no attention to this, as she thought it was Mrs. Campbell punishing Foster for not coming home. A few minutes later, Louis rushed back into the house through the front door. Louis told his mother that an automobile was parked in front of the Campbell home and that, as Louis said, "somebody must be hurt."

After Hattie Campbell tried calling for Foster to come home, she sent his older brother, Roy, who was fourteen, to look for him. Roy went to the Seventh Street hill, where most of the neighborhood children were playing. Finding no trace of Foster, Roy returned home. When Roy arrived home, Mrs. Campbell remembered the shack where Foster and the other boys played.

The shack had been built by the boys the summer before, on the north slope of the swale in which the Washington Street pumping station was located. The shack was about three hundred feet west of the pumping station and partially hidden from it by a barn. To the south, toward Liberty Street, was a meadow owned by the water company through which ran a creek. The pumping station, the shack and the meadow gate on the Seventh Street embankment, some distance to the west, were all connected by a well-beaten path through the snow. Children returning home from the Second Ward School were in the habit of cutting diagonally across the meadow from Murray Avenue to West Washington Street and passing close to the shack as they did. The boys were known to have a Wild West club, and they used the shack as their headquarters.

At about 7:00 p.m., Hattie Campbell and Roy set out for the shack. As night was falling, Roy carried a lantern. When they entered the shack, they saw Foster, who appeared to be kneeling. By the dim light of the lantern, neither Roy nor Hattie could see anything wrong. Then, as Roy reached out to touch Foster, they realized he was hanging with a rope around his neck from the roof. Hattie Campbell screamed.

"Fumbling at the knot as Roy cut the rope, the mother tore the cord away, and her screams brought her husband, who carried his still warm body to the house," reported the *Ann Arbor Daily Times News* of Friday, January 20, 1911.

"His hat was on and his coat was buttoned when we found him," said Roy later.

A Dr. M.L. Belser was notified and arrived at the house within ten minutes of receiving the call. It was most likely Dr. Belser's car that Louis saw when he told his mother "somebody must be hurt." Dr. Belser made a hasty examination of the body and declared Foster Campbell dead.

"The neck had not been broken and there was not a mark on the body except a slightly discolored ring around the neck under the chin, where the tight noose had chafed the skin," noted the account. "Dr. Belser declared that the boy had died of strangulation."

"Coroner Willis Johnson," continued the account, "who was immediately notified, viewed the remains and called an inquest for Tuesday, January 24, at 7 o'clock at Dieferié undertaking rooms."

Deputy Sheriff Freme Stark and Sergeant Thomas O'Brien were assigned to the case. Suspicion was at first directed at the playmates of Foster Campbell. The theory the officers worked with was that the boys had gone to the shack, where there was some disagreement among the boys over the question of tearing down the shack. The boys, the officers speculated, had turned on Foster during the argument and strung him up to frighten him. The boys then became frightened and fled, leaving Foster to strangle to death. Working on this theory, the officers put a number of the boys through a stiff course of questioning, but all said they had no knowledge of how Foster Campbell came to his death.

"I think maybe tramps did it," said Hattie Campbell. "Maybe he saw one and ordered him away, and the tramp turned on him. But I don't think he could have done it himself, unless it was an accident. There have been a good many tramps around here this winter."

A.R. Spokes, who was an engineer at the pumping station, said there had been only two tramps seen in the neighborhood. No one said they had seen any suspicious characters on the night Foster Campbell died.

The officers, unable to find evidence of murder, came to think that the death may have been an accident. They wondered if Foster, his head filled with Wild West stories, had arrived at the shack and experimented with the rope. The rope was already in the shack, as the boys used it to dry their gloves in between snowball fights.

"It would have been a very simple thing," noted the account,

> *to make another knot farther up the rope and form the loop by slipping the end through it. Then a stumble or a start would have tightened the second knot which would run closer to the end as it tightened with the result that the harder the boy worked the closer the knot would draw shutting off his wind. An ordinary slip knot would hardly have been so difficult for panic stricken fingers to loosen. This theory would explain the fact that there was no outcry,*

> *no disturbance until Mrs. Campbell and Roy found the little body kneeling on the rubbish. No matter if the boy had risen as he could easily have done, the cow knot would still have held. Deputy Sheriff Stark claims that the rope was tight enough around his neck to have strangled him without hanging at all.*

When L.H. Quigley, the night engineer at the pumping station, heard the news of the death of Foster Campbell, he went over to the shack and noticed the peculiar knot that had been looped around his neck. This was not a slip noose but what Mr. Quigley called a "cow knot"—a knot used by farmers to hold a cow in place.

Roy Campbell was asked, "Do you think Foster knew how to tie a knot like that?"

He answered, "No, I don't."

"It may as well be understood that with a cow knot," noted the *Ann Arbor Daily Times News* of Saturday, January 21, 1911, "a knot that will not slip after it is in place, he undoubtedly would have strangled if the knot had ever reached the tightness at which it was found. He could not possibly have released himself in time. The difficulty in accepting this solution is that a pull on a rope noosed in that manner will not cause the knot to draw tighter about the throat, but looser if anything."

"Try it," challenged the *Daily Times News*.

> *Take a soft flexible rope the size of your little finger such as strangled Foster Campbell and make a bunch of knots at one end. Fasten the other end securely. Make a loose knot some distance from the knotted end and loop the bunched knots through it. Then pull. The loose knot will draw tight around the knotted end but will remain virtually stationary with regard to the rest of the rope. One pull could not have caused a cow knot like that to run tight enough to strangle Foster Campbell. That settles the accident theory.*

To add to the mystery, on the morning of Friday, January 20, 1911, Roy Campbell and Louis Herron pointed out to Deputy Sheriff Stark a chalk scrawl on the east side of the shack. The childish scrawl was two and a half feet from the ground. The scrawl read, "Good by javel, signed Louis H."

Roy Campbell and Louis Herron both said the scrawl had not been there on the afternoon of the day before. This was confirmed by Mr. Spokes, the day engineer at the pumping station, who said it had not been there Thursday afternoon but was there Friday morning.

There was a suggestion that the message was written by Foster before he died and was missed after the discovery of the body in the darkness of evening. Roy Campbell said the message was in Foster's handwriting, but then, all nine-year-olds have scrawling handwriting. Then again, if the message was the work of Foster, what became of the chalk it was written with? No chalk was found on the body or in the area of the shack.

"In the wild west stories that the club read," noted the *Ann Arbor Daily Times News*, "the heroes undoubtedly wrote blood curdling messages that always ended '(Signed) Jack Dalton' or some other worthy. Even in the Diamond Dick series, however, it is not customary for the hero to write a good-bye message and sign some body else's name."

Who wrote the message and what it meant was never discovered.

That same morning, Coroner Johnson said, "It will bear more investigation. And it's going to be investigated, too."

The inquest into the death of Foster Campbell was to have been held on the evening of Tuesday, January 24, 1911, but it was indefinitely postponed by Coroner Willis Johnson. The jury was not discharged," explained the *Ann Arbor Daily Times News* of Wednesday, January 25, 1911, "but simply adjourned. It can be summoned at any time and the inquest held. No witnesses were subpoenaed last night."

"I am not satisfied with developments," explained Coroner Johnson.

> *I feel convinced that there is more to the case than has yet come out, and I do not intend to discharge that jury until it all does come out. All we have now is rumor and I want to say that the folks who are doing so much talking would do more good if they came through with a few facts. When the police and the sheriff's forces are ready to report, we will go ahead with the inquest. They seem to be doing about all that can be done, but I don't think we have gotten to the bottom of this and until we do I shall refuse to discharge the jury.*

There is no evidence that Coroner Johnson ever called the jury for an inquest. In the end, no one came forward to explain what had happed to Foster Campbell in the shack that evening. The police and the sheriff never got to the bottom of the mystery. The death of Foster Campbell was a puzzle in 1911 and remains a puzzle today.

9

Police Raid Fraternities

Prohibition became law in Michigan on May 1, 1918, making it illegal to commercially sell, manufacture, transport or consume alcohol in the state. National Prohibition followed on January 16, 1920. The passage of laws making the consumption of alcohol illegal did not end the thirst of those who wanted it. The closing of once legal sources of alcohol, such as bars and liquor stores, caused an inconvenience. Those who wanted alcohol badly enough to risk the consequences sought new and illegal sources. The inconvenience for those who were willing to purchase alcohol from illegal sources was an opportunity for those criminally inclined to provide it. Among those who were willing to purchase alcohol were university students, as for many, drinking was, and is, part of university life. The purchase of alcohol when it was illegal sometimes proved to have consequences.

One man who saw opportunity during Prohibition was Joseph Looney. On the night of Tuesday, February 10, 1931, Looney traveled from Detroit to Ann Arbor with a load of alcohol. Police suspected he was making such a trip and followed him. Looney, however, eluded the police. After Looney lost the police, officers picked up a man named Shirley O'Toole, who had been staying at the Hotel Huron at 200 East Huron Street in Ann Arbor, as Looney had been. O'Toole told police that Looney had delivered liquor to the five Greek letter fraternities at the University of Michigan.

Justice of the peace Bert E. Fry was called to police headquarters, which was on the same block as the Hotel Huron. At about three thirty in the morning on Wednesday, February 11, 1931, search warrants were sworn out before Justice Fry. The warrants were signed by O'Toole, who used the name Johnny Walker.

Ann Arbor police sergeants Sherman Mortenson and Norman Cook led the raids on five fraternity houses with the aid of six officers. The first house raided by police was the Kappa Sigma House at 2107 Washtenaw Avenue. There, officers confiscated fourteen quarts of whiskey, four quarts of gin and three quarts of wine. Twelve students were told to report to Justice Fry's office at ten o'clock that morning.

The next house visited by the officers was the Phi Delta Theta house at 1437 Washtenaw Avenue, where officers confiscated four quarts and nine pints of whiskey. Eighteen students were told to report to the office of Justice Fry at ten o'clock that morning.

The officers then made their way to the Delta Kappa Epsilon House at 1912 Geddes Road, where half a case of beer and four quarts of whiskey

Kappa Sigma House at 2107 Washtenaw, also known as the Hoover Residence. *Courtesy of the Bentley Historical Library, Ivory Photo Collection, Box 26.*

Phi Delta Theta House at 1437 Washtenaw. *Courtesy of the Bentley Historical Library, UM Photographs, Vertical File.*

Delta Kappa Epsilon House at 1912 Geddes. *Courtesy of the Bentley Historical Library, Ivory Photo Collection, Box 26.*

were seized. There, ten students were told to report to Justice Fry's office that morning at 10:00 a.m.

The next house to be visited by police was the Theta Delta House at 700 South State Street, where officers confiscated nine quarts of whiskey, one pint of gin and four pints of whiskey. There, twenty-two students were ordered to report to the office of Justice Fry at ten o'clock that morning.

The last house to be raided was the Sigma Alpha Epsilon House at 1408 Washtenaw Avenue, where police confiscated four quarts and one pint of liquor. There, twenty-two students were ordered to report to the office of Justice Fry at 10:00 a.m.

As police raided each house, an officer was stationed at the telephone—at that time, a house would only have one telephone—to prevent anyone from alerting other campus organizations of the raids. Officers had to borrow suitcases and grips to carry the liquor to the police station. The liquor had a retail value of about $700, and most of it had been made in Canada.

Sometime during the night, police arrested Looney, and he was taken into custody and held in the Washtenaw County Jail for violation of the Prohibition law. O'Toole was held in the jail as well, but as a witness.

Theta Delta Chi House at 700 South State Street. *Courtesy of the Bentley Historical Library, from* Michiganensian *(1931) p. 193.*

Sigma Alpha Epsilon House at 1408 Washtenaw. *Courtesy of the Bentley Historical Library, Ivory Photo Collection, Box 26.*

At ten o'clock that morning, the office of Justice Fry was filled to overflowing with some eighty-three students who had been ordered to appear before him. As they waited, Justice Fry, Washtenaw County prosecutor Albert J. Rapp, Ann Arbor chief of police Thomas M. O'Brien and Sergeant Sherman Mortenson met in conference and decided to postpone proceedings to give the police more time to conclude their investigation. A postponement of one week was agreed to. The students were then released on their own recognizance and told to appear before Justice Fry on Friday, February 20, at 10:00 a.m.

That same morning, Dr. Alexander G. Ruthven, president of the University of Michigan, issued a statement:

> *I want to commend the police officials of Ann Arbor and Washtenaw County.*
>
> *Fraternity houses here have maintained that they are organizations to a large extent independent of the University. They have pointed out that they are tax paying units and therefore are to be considered, at least in part, private houses.*

> *This attitude has been accepted by the University but with certain reservations. The right to regulate the manner in which house parties and other social events shall be conducted is retained by the University, as well as the authority to control the living conditions.*
>
> *If the fraternities are in any sense private houses and since they are tax paying institutions, they are answerable to civil authorities as well as to the University.*
>
> *Therefore, as I see it, in cases where they have collided with the law, they and not the University are answerable.*
>
> *Because the fraternities are in a real sense under the regulation of the University, they are subject to discipline by the University as well as the civil authorities.*

That evening, Washtenaw County prosecutor Albert Rapp said he had been too busy with a student bootlegging case to give careful thought to the fraternity house raids. He said he believed a more serious charge of disorderly conduct would be preferred.

An unfortunate aspect of the raids, said Rapp, was that they involved many young men who had known nothing of the liquor in the houses where they were living. These young men did not take part in drinking parties, noted Rapp. Most of these young men had been asleep when the raids were conducted and had not been drinking. They were being held on the technical charge of being in a house where liquor was found. Rapp said his office was more concerned with the apprehension of the bootleggers who had furnished the liquor found in the houses.

On the afternoon of Thursday, February 12, 1931, the committee of student affairs of the university senate was summoned to consider the matter. The committee was composed of eight faculty members and five students, who deliberated for two hours before voting to suspend the houses until September 1931. The five student members of the committee voted against the action. They were outnumbered by the members of the committee from the faculty. The committee placed the houses on social probation until September 1932. The committee had decided on its disciplinary action, electing to punish the houses as organizations rather than the specific individuals involved.

The order meant that the houses were to be closed and padlocked. Members of the fraternities who lived in the houses were ordered to move out and seek

Not everyone was unhappy at the course of events. *Courtesy of the Bentley Historical Library, from the* Gargoyle, *February 1931.*

living quarters elsewhere. Under the order, there could be no parties or other social functions sponsored by the fraternities as organizations. Further, the fraternities could not accept new members into their organizations. This placed the fraternities in a precarious financial situation because of the loss of income from the houses. The houses represented an investment of $125,000 to $175,000, on which interest had to be paid. Any repetition of the offense would result in the national councils of the fraternities being asked to withdraw the charters from the local chapters.

Not everyone agreed with the punishment dealt out to the fraternities; many saw the action of the committee as too severe. On Friday, February 13, 1936, the university student council passed a resolution asking the committee to reconsider its action and make the punishment less severe. The resolution stated:

> *The Student Council of the University of Michigan believes that the Senate Committee on Student Affairs, in punishing the five fraternities recently raided by the Ann Arbor police, acted hastily and with an unprecedented and unwarranted degree of severity and that there is indication that irrelevant considerations influenced the expressed opinions of those members who were responsible for the unnatural severity, and that no consideration was given to*

> *the unanimity of student sentiment expressed by the student members of the committee in opposition to the extreme severity of the punishment.*
>
> *In view of these circumstances the Student Council expresses itself as unalterably opposed to the severity of this punishment and recommends reconsideration by the Senate Committee on Student Affairs with regard to the closing of the fraternities from September, 1931, and further recommends reconsideration of the provision forbidding pledging and initiation during the remainder of the present school year.*

The student council had no authority in the case but submitted the resolution as an expression of opinion held by the student body.

In response to the resolution, as well as to numerous letters and telegrams from alumni petitioning the committee to reconsider its action, a special meeting of the committee was called for on Wednesday, February 18, 1931. At this meeting, the committee refused to change the action taken against the fraternities.

"Gee, you're lucky, Pete, not being a fraternity man."

Courtesy of the Bentley Historical Library, from the Gargoyle, *February 1931.*

"This *was our house.*"

Courtesy of the Bentley Historical Library, from the Gargoyle, *February 1931.*

The students who had been living in the houses finished moving out of the houses on the afternoon of Friday, February 20, 1931. That evening, the doors to the houses were locked, and they were to remain locked until September. Some 175 students were forced to find new living quarters.

The eighty-three members of the fraternities who had been ordered to appear before Justice Fry marched into his court on the morning of Friday, February 20, 1931, as ordered. Washtenaw County prosecutor Albert J. Rapp told the students that, as far as he and the police were concerned, the matter was closed. The bootleggers who had sold the liquor to the students were in jail, so no charges would be made against the students. Rapp told the students to "act as gentlemen and you will never get into trouble." Matters of discipline, he said, were up to the university. Then the students marched out of the courtroom.

At no time during the proceedings did Justice Fry enter the courtroom. "There was nothing for this court to do," Justice Fry said later. "No complaints had ever been issued against the boys, and they were not charged with the violation of any law."

Things did not go so well for Joseph Looney, who had sold the liquor to the students. He found himself standing before Washtenaw County Circuit

Court judge George W. Sample, who sentenced Looney to a term of six months to two years in prison, with the recommendation of two years.

"A man who violates any law is a queer type of American citizen," said Judge Sample. "We must protect the twenty thousand young that come into this district during the course of each year."

Prosecutor Rapp said, "It is said there is honor even among thieves and there might be among bootleggers. The booze traffic must be stopped here among the students and I deplore any person who distributes rotten, poison liquor and recommend the fullest extent of the law."

10

Betty Baker Goes on Trial

Betty Baker arrived at her home at 1804 Jackson Avenue on the afternoon of Monday, June 29, 1936, parked the car in the garage and went into the house. There, she placed a long-distance call to a family friend, Milton Schancupp, who was then an assistant in the state attorney general's office in Lansing.

"Something terrible has happened," said Mrs. Baker. "Remember some time ago I told you about trying to scare Cub? Well, I did it. I can't tell it over the phone."

Schancupp immediately drove to Ann Arbor and arrived three hours later. Betty Baker told her story. She had gone to the restaurant at 111 West Huron Street to pick up Clarence Schneider, the twenty-four-year-old boarder in the Baker home. She had given him the nickname "Cub." A quarrel broke out between the two, and Schneider called Baker a "nag."

Baker left the restaurant and went home, where she borrowed her husband's service revolver—he was an Ann Arbor police officer—without his knowledge, as he was asleep. She wrapped the gun in newspaper and returned to the restaurant. Schneider got in the back seat of the car, and Baker drove to a remote spot near the Huron River. There, she parked the car, pointed the gun at Schneider and told him not to quarrel with her in front of other people. Schneider, she said, laughed at her. As she waved the gun, it somehow went off, and the bullet struck Schneider in the face and passed through his brain. His body fell forward and came to rest in the space between the seats. Mrs. Baker then drove home and parked the car in the garage, with the body still in the backseat.

Schancupp, after listening to the story, told Mrs. Baker she should first tell her husband, Albert, what had happened and then call the police. She followed his advice and woke her husband, then called the police. She made a confession to the police, steadfastly maintaining that the shooting was an accident. She had only meant to scare him with the revolver.

"I'm going to stand by her and fight this through to the finish to clear her name," said Albert Baker. "I am convinced it was all an accident."

Mrs. Baker was thirty years of age at the time of the shooting; six years before, she had been voted the college town's most popular girl. She had been in charge of the workers in the Helen Newberry residence at the University of Michigan. Mrs. Baker had also worked as a tap dancer in Detroit and had been a drummer in a girls' band.

Betty Baker was arraigned before Justice Harry W. Reading at noon on Wednesday, July 8, 1936. "A crowd of nearly 75 persons, most of them women, jammed the justice court room at W. Huron St., no larger than a small store, for what developed to be only a routine hearing establishing the fact of the killing. All but a half dozen stood throughout the hour and a half in 100-degree temperatures," reported the *Ann Arbor Daily News* of Thursday, July 9, 1936. The justice ruled that she was to be held without bond, meaning she was to remain in jail. She was scheduled to stand trial at the October term of the circuit court on the charge of murder in the first degree.

The trial of Betty Baker was not held in the October term of the circuit court as scheduled. Because a witness was sick, the trial was postponed until January 1937. She was in the county jail all this time.

The trial was presided over by Judge George Simple, and the fate of Betty Baker was to be decided by a jury of middle-aged farmers and businessmen.

At the trial, the Washtenaw County prosecutor, Albert J. Rapp, said the shooting was deliberate and gave as the reason jealousy. Schneider, said Rapp, had been dominated by Betty Baker since he was sixteen years of age.

"She was jealous of him," said Rapp to the jury. "On the day of the murder she showed her jealousy by inquiring whether Schneider had been out with a girl because his hair was combed and his shoes shined."

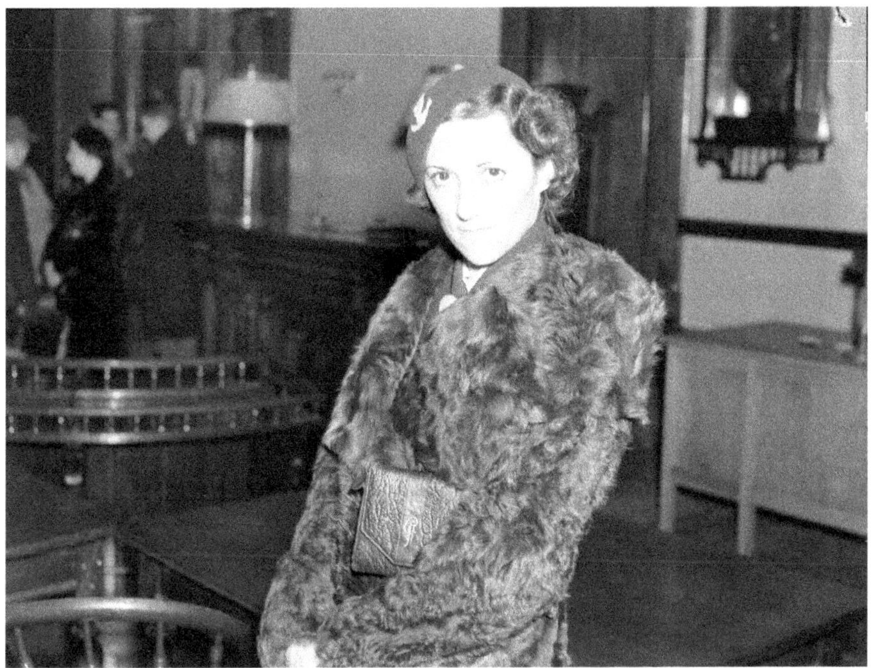

Betty Baker poses for pictures at the time of her trial, in January 1937. She had to look good for the photographers. *Courtesy of the Bentley Historical Library, Ivory Photo Collection, Box 26.*

"She made up her mind that if she couldn't have him then no one would have him," said Rapp.

Milton Schancupp was called as the first witness and told of the call he received from Betty Baker. He said he had been a friend of Mrs. Baker since 1922 and had been the attorney for the couple since 1929. Schancupp explained that Betty Baker had a "mother complex."

"She was very sympathetic and was always picking up dogs, stray cats or people who were in trouble," said Schancupp. "It seemed to be her idea to correct that lad's faults and seek to build him into a prosperous man."

"About a month before the shooting Mrs. Baker claimed that Schneider, whom she called 'Cub,' was acting tempestuously around the home and needed correction," said Schancupp. "She said she believed she could scare him into good behavior by pretending she was going to kill him. I told her the plan was silly and theatrical and advised her not to try it."

"I know she was warmly affectionate toward Cub," said Schancupp. "She was trying to cure him of bad habits, believing he contained promise."

From the time of the shooting, Betty Baker claimed the gun had discharged by accident. She said she did not intend to shoot Clarence Schneider and that the weapon went off as she flashed it. Prosecutor Rapp called Washtenaw County sheriff Jacob B. Andres, Ann Arbor chief of police Lewis W. Fohey and Officer Casper Enkemann, all of whom testified that there was no possibility of the gun discharging as Baker claimed. They demonstrated this by throwing the gun to the floor and pounding it on the arm of the witness chair.

Harold Schneider, Clarence's brother, was also called as a witness

"I met Betty at the taxicab station while her husband and Clarence were both driving cabs about eight years ago," said Harold. "The three of them ran around together. In my home last March she told me that she and my brother had fallen in love and there was no way to break it up. She said she intended to divorce Al."

"Betty said that she and Al were mismatched," continued Harold, "and that a good friend on Lansing named 'Shanty' [Betty Baker's nickname for Milton Schancupp] would fix up the divorce for her."

A couple at the trial of Betty Baker who might be Harold Schneider and his wife, Della Schneider. *Courtesy of the Bentley Historical Library, Ivory Photo Collection, Box 26.*

"She pulled out a slip of paper with some dates on it and said that Cub had not been home on these nights," testified Schneider. "She then asked me where he had been. I answered a few of the questions."

Schneider then told the court that she had used the revolver before to frighten Clarence into telling her the truth. On one occasion, Clarence had taken the gun from her, slapped her and scolded her.

"I said that Cub should have shoved the gun down her throat. I also told her that she should be ashamed of the way she was carrying on with my brother and that Al Baker was too nice a fellow to be deceived in that manner."

Another witness was Dr. Joseph H. Failing. "She came up one day about two years ago to my office and said that she was angry at someone and that he should be shot," he testified. "I said, 'Well, if you're going to shoot any one, shoot him between the eyes. That is sure death.' It was said jokingly and assumed no significance until she did shoot someone."

A Mrs. Mildred Burgett told the court that sometime before the shooting Betty Baker had come into the Kreage Dollar, where Mrs. Burgett was employed, to ask if Clarence was taking out any of the girls at the store. She told Betty Baker not at her store and suggested she ask at the dime store. Baker said she had already been there. To this, Mrs. Burgett told her to try Woolworth's. Mrs. Burgett said Betty Baker came back later and had not found anyone there who was dating Clarence.

On Thursday, January 7, 1937, Betty Baker took the stand in her own defense and in a low, calm voice told of her relationship with Clarence Schneider. Sitting in the front row was her husband, Albert, who never took his eyes off his wife. The courtroom was filled with middle-aged housewives making up most of the audience.

"I married Albert Baker in 1928 and met Cub in 1930 when Al brought home a bowling team of which he and Cub were members," said Mrs. Baker. "Both he and Al drove cabs for the same company at the time."

"How did Clarence Schneider happen to come to your home?" asked defense attorney Frank B. Devine.

Mrs. Baker responded, "My husband invited him to live with us in July 1935, because he felt sorry for Schneider, who stayed in an attic room so hot that he couldn't sleep. He came out to our place the next night and slept on the porch. He moved in his clothing in September, paying no room rent at my husband's suggestion and mine."

The two began going out together in August 1935, when they went to Walled Lake to go swimming and on the roller coaster. They returned to Ann Arbor before Albert arrived home. A week later, Betty and Clarence went for a ride to Chelsea. They went on a trip to the woods to catch polliwogs, watched wrestling matches and saw the races at Indianapolis.

"He got so he got a kick out of torturing me," said Mrs. Baker. "He would imply that he no longer loved me. By 1933, I knew that I loved him sincerely and wanted to marry him."

"It was two years after your intimacy began that you knew you loved him?" asked Prosecutor Rapp on cross-examination.

"Yes," answered Betty Baker. "I was always fond of him, though. I loved him and I loved my husband. Mr. Schneider's temperament suited me better than my husband's did."

She said she tried to talk to her husband about a divorce, but he looked pathetic and said he did not want one.

Twice before the fatal shooting of June 29, she had threatened Schneider with the gun to make him tell her the truth. "I knew he had lied to me, about things which didn't matter, but I couldn't bear to have him lie to me. Once, I took the gun and I said Cub, you are like the winds of the seven seas. You are not constant. I frightened him and he told me the truth."

On another occasion, he took the gun from her and pointed it at her. She said she dared him to pull the trigger, but he couldn't do it because he loved her. Baker told him the gun was not loaded, and they had a good laugh.

> *I went to the restaurant where he worked, and he was cross, like he had been when I threatened him with the gun before. It worked that time. I told him that I would go all to pieces if he was not kind to me. He had his shoes shined and I asked if he had been out somewhere. He called me a dammed nag.*
>
> *I went home and got the gun and wrapped it in paper. I tried to find someone to unload it, but couldn't. When we got out on the River Road in the car, I unwrapped it. He had laughed at me before because I didn't know how to handle a gun so I pulled back the hammer just to show him.*
>
> *Then I talked to him, waving the gun up and down, just for emphasis. There was an explosion I don't know whether my hand was on the trigger. I thought at first the explosion was outside. Then I saw he had fallen over. I thought he was trying to teach me a lesson.*

> *I said, "Oh don't pretend you're hurt. Don't do that." Then I saw blood. I started to drive to a hospital, but on the way it just came to me that he was dead. He didn't make a sound.*
>
> *I drove home and put the car in the garage. I told Al something terrible had happened and we must call Shanny. I wouldn't tell Al what had happened until Shanny got there. Then we called the police.*

Albert Baker took the stand on Friday, January 8, 1937, to testify on behalf of his wife, Betty. "At the outset of her incarceration, he made nightly visits to the driveway beneath her cell to pledge his loyalty. Mrs. Baker carried on the conversation through the steel gratings of her window until Sheriff Jacob B. Andrea stopped the practice," reported the *Detroit News* of Saturday, January 9, 1937. "To finance the court fight for her freedom," noted the account, "he mortgaged his interest in an Indiana estate."

Albert Baker was born in Fort Wayne, Indiana, and lived in Midland, Michigan, for seven years as a boy. In 1926, he moved to Ann Arbor, where he had various jobs until joining the Ann Arbor Police Department in 1934.

"I met Betty at the University Hospital fire in 1927," said Albert. "We were married seven or eight months later. Cub and I had been cab drivers together and I liked him. He was a member of my bowling team, and I introduced him to Betty in 1930, when I took the team to my home one evening for entertainment."

"We just got to be good friends," said Baker. "We often went out, two couples together. My wife, I believe, got Schneider dates. Sometimes I couldn't go and the others went. Nothing happened to arouse my suspicions."

"When was the first time they went out together?" asked Defense Attorney Devine.

"In the summer of 1930 they went to Walled Lake to see what kind of a place it was for a party. I couldn't go with them. Later, they went to Pleasant Lake for the same reason, and afterward Betty and I and four other couples danced there one evening. Schneider was with another girl that Betty obtained for him," said Baker.

"When did you hear for the first time that the relationship between your wife and Schneider was intimate?" asked Devine.

"In this court," answered Baker, biting his lip.

"You had no previous inkling?" asked Devine

"Not until two days after the shooting, when Harold Schneider said my wife told him of her thoughts of divorcing me and marrying Cub."

"When did Mrs. Baker talk with you of a divorce?" continued Devine.

"I don't remember when it was. She said her nerves were shot and wondered if I wanted a divorce. I told her no, we were happy and I didn't know of any grounds at the time. On the evening of the shooting, my wife refused to tell me what had happened until Shanty arrived. She was upset and excited and I knew something was wrong. When Shanty got there, she said she had killed Cub."

"The news almost knocked me off my feet," continued Baker.

On the evening of Friday, January 8, 1937, he had been relieved of his duties on the Ann Arbor Police Force by the Police Commission. No reason was given by the commission for this action. "The action of the commission came a few hours after a disturbance in court yesterday afternoon when Baker seized plates from a Detroit photographer and destroyed them. The camera man had snapped Baker during a recess," reported the *Ann Arbor News* of Saturday, January 9, 1937.

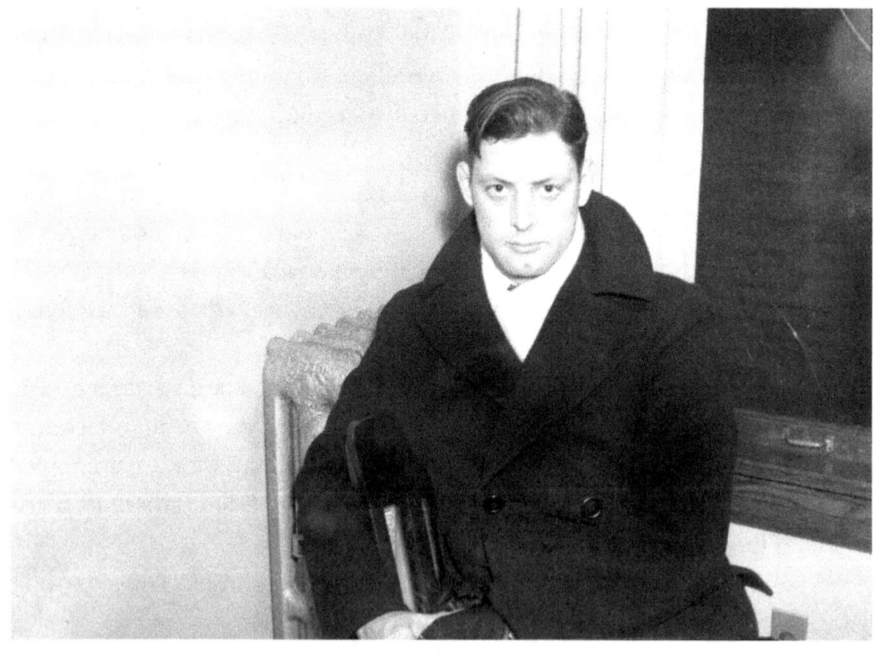

Albert Baker poses for photographers at the time of the trial. He stood behind his wife from the beginning to the end. *Courtesy of the Bentley Historical Library, Ivory Photo Collection, Box 26.*

"Later," continued the paper, "the husband of the defendant agreed to pose for pictures for two Detroit photographers including the one with whom he had struggled earlier."

The trial came to a close on Monday, January 11, 1937, as each side made a final summation before the jury. As they did, the corridors outside the courtroom were packed with people, held back by bailiffs and police officers.

"It has been testified that she said that her husband was all right to support her, but that when it came to love she wasn't going to lose that man," said Prosecutor Rapp, as he summed up the case for the jury.

> *She had testified that she loved him. If she couldn't have him no one was going to have him. She could not have known he was dead when she left him lying in the garage. Would any reasonable person have done that in case of an accidental shooting?*
>
> *Less than nine months after her marriage she was having an affair with Cub. Here is her husband, who has stood by her, yet she trampled down and made a fool of him. She is a woman who must have what she wants at any cost. Jealousy was the motive of this shooting.*

The defense made its last argument as well. "She never had malice in her heart," said Devine. "This man who has been pictured as an inexperienced boy, this Schneider, was a taxi drive. Taxi drivers are not the most innocent class of people in the world. Time and again he had threatened to commit suicide if she left him. Once he had attempted it. There was no jealousy here."

The case was turned over to the jury, which could decide on one of four verdicts: murder in the first degree, murder in the second degree, manslaughter or acquittal. At 5:25 p.m. on Tuesday, January 12, 1937, the jury returned a verdict of guilty in the second degree. Judge George Sample passed a sentence of life imprisonment at the Detroit House of Corrections. This was the maximum Baker could receive. She would be eligible for parole in fifteen years.

Betty Baker was driven to her new home, the Detroit House of Corrections, on Wednesday, January 14, 1937. "Six miles from her future home," reported the *Ypsilanti Daily Press*, "the car containing Mrs. Baker was overtaken by that of her husband Albert K. Baker, and of his sister, Mrs. Jessie Robart, of Fort Wayne, Ind. Baker waved his farewell having missed seeing his wife before she left Ann Arbor."

11

Ann Arbor Police Gambling Scandal

Washtenaw County Circuit Court judge James R. Breakey Jr. held a press conference just after noon on Tuesday, June 11, 1946. Judge Breakey had just finished a yearlong investigation into gambling in the city of Ann Arbor as a one-man grand jury, with Prosecutor William Brusstar assisting. At the press conference, Judge Breakey called for the removal of Ann Arbor police chief Sherman Mortenson and detective lieutenant Eugene Gehringer. Breakey charged Mortenson and Gehringer with malfeasance, misfeasance, willful neglect of duty and other offenses. The two, Breakey charged, had accepted bribes and protection money and knowingly permitted gamblers to operate in the city of Ann Arbor. He requested that the board of police commissioners take all legal steps to have both men removed from office.

"Judge Breakey said neither Gehringer nor Mortenson had been indicted by the grand jury," reported the *Ann Arbor News* of Tuesday, June 11, 1946. "He declined to comment when asked if they would be."

That evening, the board of police commissioners suspended Mortenson and Gehringer. Police captain Casper Enkemann was appointed by the board as acting chief. The board named Sergeant Albert Heusel as acting head of the detective bureau. After they were suspended, both Mortenson and Gehringer demanded a hearing before the commission on their suspensions.

After the meeting, board member Orlando Stephenson said, "This is the first time anything like this has happened here. We naturally are deeply shocked, but we have sworn to do our duty and will let the ax fall where it may, whether it hurts anyone or not."

At the time, Sherman Mortenson was forty-five years old, having been born on a farm near Pinckney. He was educated in the Ann Arbor school. He had joined the Ann Arbor Police Department in 1923 as a patrolman and had worked his way up through the ranks. He succeeded Norman Cook as chief on July 5, 1941.

Gehringer had joined the Ann Arbor Police Department in 1927 and had been a detective for twelve years. He had been head of the detective bureau since 1941.

The next morning, Mortenson issued a statement:

> *Of course I am shocked at these general charges and accusations which I most earnestly and emphatically deny.*
>
> *I have been an officer of the law for 23 years and have felt that I have earned and deserved the confidence and respect of my associates in this community.*
>
> *It has been my experience as a peace officer that even the most desperate law violator is entitled to his opportunity for a fair, impartial and just hearing. I shall expect no more and will be satisfied with no less.*
>
> *Until the time arrives I shall have nothing further to say except that I trust my friends will still keep on indicating their confidence and faith in me as they have so generously done since this publicity was created.*

The police commission began hearings against Mortenson and Gehringer in the city council chambers on August 4, 1946. The hearings were to determine the status of employment of the two men with the department. Mortenson and Gehringer had not been charged with any criminal offense.

At the hearing on the afternoon of August 6, 1946, Attorney Louis E. Burke read a statement on behalf of his client, Sherman Mortenson, informing the commission of his decision to resign the office of chief of police.

"I have no intention of resuming my former position in the [police] department in any capacity," read the statement. In the statement, Mortenson declared that "it would be unjust to myself and to the men in the department" if he resumed his duties as chief. He said the men working under him would be subject to "unfair suspicion and with that handicap they, too, would be unable to do their best work."

"Nothing that I could do," he said, "would convince certain people who desired to think otherwise that I was trying to do an honest, efficient and capable job."

This action took place twenty-three years to the day after his appointment to the Ann Arbor Police Department.

Burke, who read the statement, said he hoped the hearing would continue but would now be confined to the alleged bribery.

"Special Grand Jury Prosecutor William Brusstar objected strenuously," reported the *Ann Arbor News* of Tuesday, August 6, 1946, "saying that he had 'arranged the case in one way' and that if the bribery were considered, without the other charges, he would be unable to proceed with the case."

Ralph Keyes, attorney for Gehringer, said he saw no reason why the hearing could not go on, unless the statement from Mortenson was an admission of guilt.

Burke said the statement definitely was not an admission of guilt. The commission then agreed to continue as planned, considering all charges.

That afternoon, the council chambers were about two-thirds full with spectators. The three commissioners were seated at adjoining desks set on a raised platform at the front of the room. Commission chairman Orlando W. Stephenson was seated at the center with commissioner Joseph C. Hooper to his left and commissioner Herbert L. Frisinger to his right. City attorney William M. Laird sat to Hooper's left to give advice to the commission on legal questions.

In front of the commissioners sat grand jury prosecutor William Brusstar with the grand jury special investigator Gordon Gillis. Chief Mortenson and his attorney, Louis Burke, sat to the left of the commissioners, while Gehringer and his attorney, Ralph Keyes, sat at a desk to the right of the commissioners. In front of the commissioners were the witness chair and the recorder's desk.

That afternoon, George Whitman, former owner of a poolroom at 119 East Ann Street, said he had given Gehringer about fifty dollars over a period of approximately six months. Whitman said the money was paid in lots of ten dollars and was just a present and had never been solicited. He said he had asked Gehringer if it was permissible to play cards in the poolroom. According to Whitman, Gehringer had said it was all right if no money was involved.

Under cross-examination, Whitman said he had once rented two parking spaces at the Armory from Gehringer, who was then a member of the Army Reserve, and had once rented the Armory for a club meeting. Keyes, attorney for Gehringer, claimed the money was rental payment. Brusstar countered that all rentals were paid by check, but he was unable to produce the checks. Whitman said he did not intend the money to be rental payments.

On Wednesday, August 7, 1946, three clerks who had been employed at the United Cigar Store testified that they had handled some $1,500 a day in local bets on horse races and another $7,000 to $8,000 in relay operations over the telephone. Witnesses described a basement room with form sheets and race entry lists, where the public could place bets. There was also a "hooligan" dice game that had been maintained off and on in an upstairs room.

Patrolman Joseph Huizenga testified that in 1945, Chief Mortenson had told him, "There is no sense in bothering with gambling at the United Cigar Store. If you stop gambling in one place it will just start up in another."

Burke rapped Huizenga for not pursuing his complaint of gambling with the commission or some other agency. Huizenga had previously said he had forgotten about it after being told not to brother.

A second officer, Walter Krasny, testified that he had reported gambling at the store to then Sergeant Enkemann, but no action was taken. Krasny said he had no personal evidence of gambling at the store but had been informed by friends that bets were being accepted there.

Detective George Stauch told the commission he had once been told by Gehringer that gambling was small and petty and the detective bureau "had more important things to watch." Stauch told the commission that Mortenson had never told him to "lay off" any reputed gambling place: "The chief never told me to lay off anything."

Stauch said that on one occasion, he asked Washtenaw County prosecutor John W. Rea for a search warrant for a house on Catherine Street.

"I had a complaint of gambling and illegal liquor sales there," said Stauch, "but Rea refused the warrant for 'insufficient evidence.'"

Stauch then approached assistant prosecutor Leonard Young, who told Stauch there was "plenty of evidence." Rea still refused to obtain a search warrant. A few days later, Mortenson obtained a search warrant.

The subsequent raid resulted in no arrests. Stauch testified that the full platoon of officers who visited the house found no "gamblers or gambling" and no liquor. "No records of the raid could be found in police files, Stauch said," reported the *Ann Arbor News* on Thursday, August 8, 1946.

John M. Jetter, owner of the United Cigar Store until June 1940, said he had paid Gehringer between $10 and $20 a month between 1938 and 1940. This money, Jetter said, was not paid for protection from police raids. He said he never had a bargain or agreement concerning gambling with Gehringer. Jetter told the commission that he paid the money to Gehringer to collect on bad checks cashed at the store. Jetter claimed the store cashed about $1,500 in checks daily, and some of them bounced. He then gave the bad checks to Gehringer, who collected on the checks, and Jetter in turn rewarded Gehringer for this service.

Nick Theros, possibly the head of gambling operations in Ann Arbor, was called as a witness before the commission. Prosecutor William Brusstar, early on the afternoon of Thursday, August 8, 1946, asked Theros, "Did you, in 1941 and 1942, when in the numbers business, pay any protection money to Chief Mortenson?"

Theros had been warned by commission chairman Joseph Hooper that he would be granted immunity only on questions of gambling and not on questions of bribery.

Theros refused to answer the question, as he feared he would incriminate himself.

Special investigator Gordon Gillis said he would procure a new grant of immunity from Judge Breakey Jr. Gillis told the commission he would present the grant to the commission the next morning.

"The immunity grant means simply that an individual may implicate himself in illegal acts without fear of subsequent arrest. Once having been declared immune, he may be forced to answer any question concerning the acts covered," explained the *Ann Arbor News* of Friday, August 9, 1946.

"Michigan statutes," continued the *Ann Arbor News*, "provide that a prosecuting attorney may request an order of immunity during the interrogation of a witness. The presiding judge may then issue the grant at his own discretion, after which it becomes a matter of public record."

By this time, the hearing was coming to a close, but Brusstar had called only twelve of the forty witnesses he had listed. Brusstar explained that he did not intend to use all of the witnesses. Burke asked for the names of those who would be called.

To this, Brusstar said, "All right, I'm going to call Theros, and he's going to say he bribed Mortenson."

"He will not," responded Burke. "Not unless you browbeat him into saying so." Burke then added that he had heard someone had drawn a pistol on Theros during a night grand jury session.

Brusstar called the accusation "preposterous" and added, "I have never listened to a wilder statement."

When Theros did testify before the commission, on Friday, August 9, 1946, he said he had paid Mortenson between $180 and $4,200 during the years 1941 and 1942. The money, said Theros, was paid in lots of $25 to $50 on five or six occasions.

"Under cross-examination he was unable to state where the money was exchanged and admitted he had no agreement with Chief Mortenson for any protection. It was further revealed he was under a psychiatrist care during the time frame that he allegedly gave the chief the money. Theros testified he was never threatened with a gun, as alleged by Defense Attorney Burke, but that County Prosecutor Rea wore one once, when he was being questioned by him," noted the online history of the Ann Arbor Police Department.

Once the questioning of Theros was completed, Brusstar rested his case. The other side of the story began on Saturday, August 10, 1946, when Burke called Mortenson to the stand. Under questioning, Mortenson denied that he took money to protect gamblers in Ann Arbor. He said he never closed his eyes to the gambling situation in Ann Arbor. "Department records show there definitely was something done about it."

When questioned about the money Theros said he gave him, Mortenson said, "I never took money from Theros or anyone else."

He admitted to receiving baskets of fruit twice at Christmas from Theros, adding that he received "innumerable" gifts from townspeople and business firms each holiday season. Mortenson said he knew Theros "only to speak to on the street."

Mortenson said he never told Officer Huizenga that "there is no sense bothering with gambling at the United Cigar Store. Joe [Huizenga] never brought me a gambling complaint about the cigar store, and I never ordered him or any other officer to lay off any gambling place."

Mortenson said he was aware of the reputation of the United Cigar Store but never made a personal investigation or questioned any of the employees.

Brusstar, during cross-examination, asked Mortenson about Dan Raftopolous, who was arrested for gambling but let off with a warning to "cut it out."

"Why didn't you take similar steps against other known gamblers?" asked Brusstar.

Mortenson said he didn't know. He said he had issued orders to have gambling places watched and ordered arrests when there was sufficient evidence.

Mortenson was the only witness called by Burke.

On Tuesday, August 13, 1946, Gehringer took the stand in his own defense.

"The detective," reported the *Ann Arbor News* of the same day, "denounced each specific accusation made in 10 pages of findings submitted to the police commission by Circuit Judge James R. Breakey, Jr. He vehemently disclaimed ever having taken bribes to protect gambling interests."

"Replying to charges of bribery and neglect of duty as substantiated by prosecution witnesses," continued the *Ann Arbor News*, "Gehringer's statements on the stand became a monotonous succession of negatives and denials. He claimed he had always fully done his duty as a police officer."

Gehringer said he always made gambling arrests "when I had the evidence" and "never protected anyone."

He admitted he knew Wilson C. Haight, part owner of the United Cigar Store, but denied being a close friend. Gehringer admitted, as well, to having played cards "for small stakes" with Haight at the United Cigar Store. He also admitted to receiving small amounts of money from John Jetter, the former owner of the United Cigar Store, but claimed the money was for collecting money owed for bad checks. He said that was a service he performed for other businesses and townspeople.

Gehringer was asked about a statement he purportedly made to Detective George Stauch that gambling was "small and petty" and "not as important as other duties." He denied making the statement but admitted that he told Stauch not to make lengthy investigations into gambling when working on other cases.

During cross-examination, Brusstar produced seven written reports from Gehringer to Mortenson, stating in each case but one that no evidence of gambling was found.

Gehringer was the only witness called for his defense.

The hearing was finished; now the commission needed time to consider its conclusions.

The police commission handed down its decision on Thursday, August 22, 1946, nine days after finishing the hearings. The commission cleared Sherman Mortenson of all charges brought against him by the grand jury. Detective Lieutenant Eugene Gehringer was ordered removed from the department because of improper, but not criminal, conduct.

Concerning Mortenson, the commission concluded:

> *1. That there is not a clear and satisfactory preponderance of the evidence produced at the hearing before this commission to sustain the charge that Sherman H. Mortenson accepted money, directly or indirectly, from underworld characters or employees of unlawful and illegal enterprises.*
>
> *2. That the written statement signed by Sherman H. Mortenson, and filed and read into the record at the commencement of the proceedings before the commission, is equivalent to a resignation, and the same is hereby so considered by the commission, because Sherman H. Mortenson therein advised this commission that he has no intention of resuming his former position in the department in any capacity.*
>
> *It is therefore ordered that the employment of Sherman H. Mortenson as a member of the Ann Arbor Police Department be terminated as of August 6, 1946.*

Concerning Gehringer, the commission concluded:

> *1. That by undisputed testimony, we find that Eugene J. Gehringer accepted sums of money from a person then connected with gambling in the claim that such money was for services rendered in collecting worthless checks, when it was known by Eugene J. Gehringer that such services could not be rendered by any member of the Department for compensation, and was rendered to others for compensation.*
>
> *2. That it was known by Eugene J. Gehringer as lieutenant of the Detective Division, that it was the function of his department to investigate gambling and that notwithstanding such knowledge, he had associations and connections with individuals, who were involved in gambling activities, which associations and connections disqualified him insofar as his usefulness to the Department is concerned.*

> *3. That in giving instructions to a subordinate in his department, namely, the Detective Division, he made it appear that gambling in the City of Ann Arbor was of minor consequence and that it was not necessary to give it primary attention, when he himself knew that the enforcement of the laws with respect to gambling was a matter of major consequence.*
>
> *It is ordered therefore that Eugene J. Gehringer is hereby removed from the Ann Arbor Police Department for the reasons above stated, as of the date of his suspension, to-wit: June 11, 1946.*

Once the findings of the commission were released, both Mortenson and Gehringer issued statements of their own.

Mortenson stated, "I felt throughout that there was no other decision the commission could make. I knew in my own mind that I had nothing in my record of 23 years as police officer and chief for which I must apologize."

Gehringer stated that the vindication on the sweeping charges of bribery, corruption, conspiracy and association with underworld figures was gratifying. He noted that the testimony reflected the absence of misconduct on his part.

> *The finding that I had disqualified myself in so far as my usefulness to the department is concerned is hardly borne out by the record. My undisputed testimony is that I did have gambling as well as all law violations under constant surveillance and would and did make arrests for gambling when such violations occurred in my presence and in such manner that the arrests would be sustained in a court of record. No other instructions were ever given by me to my subordinate officers.*
>
> *The decision reached is a harsh one, under the circumstances and on the testimony adduced. However, it has been foremost in my mind since the grand jury findings were made public that my usefulness to the Ann Arbor police department was then so seriously impaired that it would have been impossible for me to have continued in my official capacity, regardless of the commission's decision.*
>
> *My sole purpose throughout the entire hearing was to clear my name of the claimed bribery and corruption. That has been done.*

No criminal charges were ever brought against Mortenson or Gehringer. The Ann Arbor Police gambling scandal had come to an end

12

Death of a Nurse

The Case of William Morey

Christian Helmut, his wife Lois and their friends Mr. and Mrs. Holwerda were returning to the Helmut home on Washington Heights in Ann Arbor after having seen a movie. He turned the car onto the dark, tree-lined street and proceeded toward the house. As they neared the Helmut home just after midnight on Monday, September 17, 1951, they passed the house at 1424 Washington Heights. They saw an object in the street near the curb. Helmut thought the object was a blanket. The two couples arrived at the Helmut home, and Christian and Mr. Holwerda walked back to see what the object was. The two men found the body of a young woman.

Helmut ran to the nearby home of Raymond Cook, a policeman, but was unable to rouse anyone. Officer Cook was on duty at the time. Returning to the body, Helmut, a first-year medical student, felt what he thought was a faint pulse. He then ran back to his home and called police. Police soon after arrived, and the woman was taken in the Sheriff's Department ambulance to St. Joseph's Mercy Hospital, then on Ingalls, between Cornwell and Catherine Streets. The woman was declared dead on arrival. It is possible that the woman was identified at this time as Pauline Ada Campbell, a nurse employed at the hospital.

Pauline Ada Campbell was described as a pretty thirty-four-year-old woman who was said to have been shy, quiet, modest, faithful, cooperative and hard to get to know. Her landlady, Mrs. Ivan L. Weldemier, said she was "quiet, modest and neat as a pin."

"She had no callers and received little mail," said Mrs. Weldemier. "She'd lived with us more than a year, but we knew hardly anything about her. She spent most of her time doing needlework in her room."

Pauline Campbell was born in Ohio, and her parents died when she was a child. She was raised by Mr. and Mrs. Asa C. Elsea on a family farm near Alma. Campbell attended Ann Arbor High School, graduating in 1944. She graduated from the St. Lawrence Hospital School of Nursing in Lansing in 1947 and became a registered nurse.

She returned to Ann Arbor and took a job at the University Maternity Hospital, where she was employed from 1947 to March 1950. Campbell then went to St. Joseph's Mercy Hospital, where she was employed in the nursery. At the time of her murder, she was in charge of taking care of babies.

St. Joseph's Mercy Hospital was once on Ingalls Street in Ann Arbor. *Courtesy of the Bentley Historical Library, Ivory Photo Collection, Box 2.*

Nurse Campbell finished her shift at St. Joseph's Mercy Hospital and left for home at about 11:50 p.m. on Sunday, September 16, 1951. She walked the ten blocks to the boardinghouse where she lived in about fifteen minutes. There, just as she arrived at the front of the house, she was struck twice on the side of the head with a heavy metallic object. One blow struck Miss Campbell behind the right ear, and the second hit her in the region of the right temple. The force of the blows was enough to dislodge the brain. A pool of blood was found on the sidewalk in front of her boardinghouse. The killer then dragged her body some twenty feet into the street. The body was left behind a car parked in front of the house. Police wondered if the killer planned to hide the body in a nearby field or tried to make the murder look like a hit-and-run accident. There had been no sexual assault.

When she was murdered, Campbell was carrying a paper bag containing a thermos bottle and a jar of instant coffee, as well as a second empty paper bag in which she had most likely carried her lunch. Missing from the body was a red leather purse she usually carried.

Shirley Ferguson, who lived in a third-floor room in the same boardinghouse as Miss Campbell, told police she was awakened at 12:04 a.m. by what she thought was the sound of running footsteps. She said "they sounded like a woman's."

"I was half asleep when the noise woke me up. I looked at my watch and then heard in succession what I believe was a low moan, men's voices, a car door slam, then the car starting off very fast," said Miss Ferguson.

Ann Arbor Police noted that the pattern of the murder of Nurse Campbell fit the assaults on two other nurses and an attempt on a third only a few blocks from where Campbell was killed. Nurse Mary Jane McWherter was hit on the head and pushed into a patch of shrubbery on the 900 block of East Ann Street early on the morning of May 14, 1951. McWherter told police that her attacker stumbled and fell as he ran away. Police found a rock about the size of a baseball where he fell. The attacker, police concluded, used the rock on McWherter and dropped it as he fell.

On the Tuesday before Miss Campbell's murder, Nurse Shirley N. Mackley was struck on the head near Couzens Hall on Ann Street. At the time, she was walking toward University Hospital. She suffered deep lacerations on her scalp. Her screams drove her attacker away. She told police she thought she had been struck with a pipe wrench.

On the night of the murder, and at about the same time, Frances Elyea, night supervisor at University Hospital, told police she was chased by a man near the Pemberton Welsh Nurses Residence. She saw the man approach her and fled into a nearby residence.

Ann Arbor chief of police Casper M. Enkemann took personal command of the investigation, assigning thirty officers to the case. "The odds against catching the killer are growing as time elapses," said Chief Enkemann. "We have received a great many tips, and every one of them is being investigated. We have asked for and received the cooperation of the State Police and sheriff's department and also have had help from police in Detroit, Chicago, Flint, Trenton and Ypsilanti."

Police had few clues as they began their investigation. Some thirty-five suspects were questioned by police, but they made little progress. Among those questioned was William Montgomery, a friend of Campbell's and perhaps her closest friend. The two had dated on and off for fourteen years and had talked of marriage, but in the end they were just good friends. Montgomery had been at the Elks Club from 11:00 p.m. until 2:30 a.m. He said he last saw Campbell a week before her death. "She was afraid that something like this would happen," said Montgomery. "She told me several times she was frightened to walk through those dark streets between her house and the hospital. But she usually walked. She almost never took a cab."

Police began by questioning known sexual deviants in Washtenaw County on the possibility that the killer might be psychotic.

"The heinous act was the work of someone who apparently has a compulsion or phobia delusion against nurses or women," explained Dr. O.R. Yoder, the medical superintendent of the Ypsilanti State Hospital and a psychiatrist, to the *Ann Arbor News* on Tuesday, September 18, 1951. "If this is true then we can certainly expect him to make a similar murder attempt in the future."

"But this theory," Yoder added, "is based upon the assumption that the killer is psychotic or an unbalanced individual." Yoder noted that it was unusual for sex deviants to change their behavior patterns. "In other words," said Yoder, "the deviant seldom goes from the window peeping of assault phase to an act such as murder or other forms of deviation."

Police did learn that the report of an attempted assault on Frances Elyes on the night of the murder had nothing to do with the killing of Pauline

Campbell. A young man had come forward to tell police he was the man Elyes thought was chasing her. The young man explained that he was approaching the building to meet a nurse he was to escort to her home; he stumbled against a rock, causing him to step quickly forward several feet as he regained his balance. The young man saw Elyes turn and run to a nearby residence.

At the University Hospital, male graduate students formed an escort service to protect nurses moving from the hospital and its auxiliary units and their homes. Arrangements were made to transport night duty nurses between their homes and the hospital. A cab company volunteered its services to transport night duty nurses as they went from home to work free of charge.

Even after fifty possible suspects had been questioned, the police found they were no further along in the investigation then when they began. Ann Arbor mayor William E. Brown offered a reward of $500 for information leading to the arrest and conviction of the killer. "I believe someone besides the killer knows his identity," said Mayor Brown. "This horrible crime must be solved as quickly as possible. We fear that as time passes persons who have important information will be more reluctant to divulge it. Therefore, we appeal to them to come forward now."

Ann Arbor police detective Duane Bauer was weary after hours of running down leads in the Campbell case that evaporated into nothing. Some fifty suspects had been questioned with no result, and some fifty more remained to be questioned. Then, at 3:00 p.m. on Wednesday, September 19, 1951, Sergeant Howard Remnant went into the detective bureau to tell Bauer, "There's someone out here who wants to see a detective."

Detective Bauer told Remnant to tell whoever it was to wait a couple minutes until an interview room was free for use. When Bauer saw the rooms were to be in use for some time, he went into the hall. There he saw Daniel Baughey in the main corridor of the Ann Arbor City Hall, near the staircase. Bauer asked Baughey what he wanted.

"I'm positive I know who slugged the nurse who wasn't killed," answered Baughey. (This was Shirley Mackley, who was attacked on September 12 near Couzens Hall, three days before Campbell was murdered.)

Bauer took Baughey by the arm and led him into the detective bureau fast. An interview room was cleared, and Baughey repeated his statement about the Mackley assault. Baughey said he suspected William Morey and Max Pell, both of Ypsilanti, of assaulting Mackley.

Baughey told Bauer that he had been talking with his friend William Morey two days after the assault on Mackley. Baughey said to Morey that he had read in the newspaper about a nurse getting slugged in Ann Arbor that Tuesday.

To this, Morey said, "You know who did that. Well, you're looking at him." Then Morey showed Baughey an eight-inch crescent wrench, with which Morey said he had assaulted Mackley.

"You should have heard her yell," Baughey quoted Morey as saying. "It was the funniest thing I ever heard. I laughed so hard about her screaming I could hardly drive away"

Baughey thought Morey was boasting until he saw Morey and Pell after Campbell's murder. He saw Morey and Pell in the Fifth Wheel, a restaurant near Ypsilanti.

"Everybody in the place was talking about the murder," said Baughey. "Bill and Max were looking at a paper. When they saw me, they threw it down and tried to avoid me. He didn't want to talk to me this time. He wasn't the same."

Baughey went to talk to his father, the minister at the Evangelistic Mission Tabernacle Church, and told him he suspected Morey and Pell.

"There is nothing for you to do but go the police," said his father. "It is your duty."

Detectives went to Ypsilanti and arrested Morey at his home and Pell at a garage where he was employed. At the same time, police arrested David Royal of Milan, a construction worker, because he was a frequent companion of Morey and Pell. The brutal murder of Campbell had shocked the community; now, the ages of the suspects would bring another shock. Morey and Pell were eighteen years of age, and Royal was seventeen years of age. The three were taken to the jail at Ypsilanti, where they were confronted by Baughey. All three laughed when told they were suspected of the murder of Pauline Campbell. The three were asked if they agreed to go to State Police Headquarters in East Lansing, where they could take a lie detector test.

"We don't believe in lie tests," said Morey.

"I do," said Baughey. "I'll take a test. I'll show I'm telling the truth."

At this, Morey, Pell and Royal agreed to take the test if Baughey did. Then the trip to East Lansing began.

Ann Arbor Chief of Police Enkemann rode in a car with Pell. Pell's car, a 1948 coup, was driven by another officer. Pell was worried about his car because it was being driven at over sixty miles an hour.

"I just put a new motor in," said Pell. "I don't want it hurt."

The cars stopped near East Lansing, and the officer driving Pell's car told Chief Enkemann that he had seen spots in the car that he believed to be bloodstains.

"We'll rip out that upholstery and have it tested," said Enkemann.

"You'll spoil my car!" screamed Pell. "Don't do that!"

"Why don't you come clean then?" said Enkemann to Pell. "Tell us what happened."

"I guess I should," answered Pell. "Only I don't want the other guys sore at me."

"Then we'll have to rip your car to pieces," said Enkemann. The car, Enkemann realized, was Pell's prized possession.

As they walked into the State Police Headquarters, Pell said, "We did it. But we didn't mean to kill her. We wanted money for gasoline."

Within an hour of their arrival in Lansing, Royal and Morey had confessed as well. The lie detector tests were never taken.

To Enkemann, Morey said, "Baughey is going to be an unpopular guy around Ypsi."

Enkemann asked Morey if he would rather have gone through life with this on his conscience.

Morey answered, "Well, Baughey lied. I didn't laugh about the assaults, except at the Normal College the other day when we were talking to a group of students.

"Some girl said something about how she would run if she ever saw the guy who killed the nurse, and I wondered what she would do if she knew I did it, and I laughed."

All three told the same story of the events of that night. The three had dates with Ann Arbor girls and had purchased a case of beer at the Ideal Tavern in Milan, "where they didn't ask questions." The three said they were "a little drunk." Once the three had dropped the girls off at their homes, Pell, who was driving, said he needed gas money. They decided to rob someone for gas and beer money. They also chose to rob a nurse, as nurses are on the streets late and walk alone.

As they drove near St. Joseph's Mercy Hospital, they saw a woman in a white uniform walking on Observatory. Morey told Pell to stop the car and got out, taking a rubber mallet with him. Pell had taken the mallet from the garage where he was employed. The mallet, made of hard rubber, was used to remove dents from cars and change tires; it had an eighteen-inch handle and a head five inches across. Holding the mallet in his hand, Morey followed Campbell as she crossed Observatory and began walking on Washington Heights. Pell turned out the lights of the car and followed Morey.

"She didn't even know I was behind her," said Morey. "I ran on the grass to catch up and hit her twice on the back of the head. She dropped on the sidewalk. I dragged her to the curb and when Max came up, Dave got out and we started to push her in the car."

Morey held Campbell by the arms, and Royal had hold of her legs as the two carried her to the side of the car. Campbell was still alive and breathing hard. Pell cried out, "Hey! You'll get blood on my car."

Morey and Royal dropped Campbell in the street, and Morey grabbed her red purse. Then they got in the car, and the three drove away. They removed the money from the purse, a total of $1.50, and put the purse in the glove compartment.

The three drove down Observatory and then turned on to Geddes Road. They tossed the purse into the Huron River from the bridge on Superior Road.

"We did it for the money," Morey later explained. "We needed gasoline, and we might have had more beer if we got enough. That was the only reason."

The three used the money to purchase gasoline in Ypsilanti and then drove back to Ann Arbor on Packard Road. Near Ann Arbor, they saw a police roadblock stopping cars leaving Ann Arbor. As they were driving into Ann Arbor, they were neither stopped nor questioned.

"It's a good thing, too," said Pell later. "We had that bloody hammer in the backseat."

After riding around Ann Arbor for a time, they went out Packard Road to radio station WHRV, where the three attended a lawn program. Then they went home.

The murder of Pauline Campbell had sent shock waves through the community. Now, the arrest of Morey, Pell and Royal sent a new series of shock waves through the community, as they seemed like such nice boys from good families.

"The whole thing seems like a 'Dr. Jekyll and Mr. Hyde' affair to me," said the father of William Morey, also named William Morey. "There has never been any trouble in the family before. It's hard to understand."

The father noted that his handsome son was popular with girls and had shown no signs of wildness until Max Pell had returned from a trip to the South. Then, young Morey had started staying out late.

The young Morey was a member of the Naval Air Reserve and had just completed eight weeks of training at Grosse Ile. Morey had used the money he earned to enroll as a freshman at the Michigan State Normal College, now Eastern Michigan University. While at Ypsilanti High School, Morey had been a B student and had played on the tennis team.

The young William Morey had been arrested by police in Ann Arbor on March 11, 1951. He had bought some beer and driven to Ann Arbor. Morey and his friends were charged with disorderly conduct and released.

Max Pell was an only child who had dropped out of Roosevelt High School in March. His grades had been good, and he had been on the football and track teams. Then he started skipping classes. He had gone south looking for work but returned after a few weeks. Then he had gone to Oregon, where he had worked in a lumber camp. On his return to Ypsilanti, he had found employment in a garage.

Pell had been arrested by the Michigan State Police on a charge of stealing gasoline on September 4, 1951. He pleaded guilty and paid a fine of $14.30 and costs. Pell had been arrested by police in Ypsilanti when he was sixteen, on April 4, 1951, for leaving the scene of an accident. He was released and turned over to his parents.

"I don't care whether it's my boy or not," said the foster father of David Royal. "When he gets into a thing like this, he should be made to pay."

His mother described David Royal as a "quiet, obedient boy."

David Royal had dropped out of high school in his sophomore year and joined the navy. He received a medical discharge after twenty-eight days because of a knee disability.

"We never had anything against him but traffic violations," said Milan police chief Tom Goodrich, "but the way he was going we figured he was heading for trouble."

Royal had been arrested with Pell by the Michigan State Police on a charge of stealing gasoline but was released after questioning. The Michigan State Police had arrested Royal again on September 4, on suspicion of stealing articles from cars parked at the Kaiser-Frazer Corp. parking lot at Willow Run, but again, he was released.

When told of the arrest and his confession to the Campbell murder, Mrs. Royal sobbed and said, "It can't be true."

The brutal murder of Pauline Campbell had shocked the Ann Arbor community to its core, as it was a city with little violent crime. What stunned the community even further was the lack of remorse expressed by the three perpetrators.

The trial of the three began at the end of October 1951 with jury selection. The presiding judge was James Breakey. In early November, the trial itself began, when Washtenaw County prosecutor Douglas K. Reading read the statements of the three into the record. As part of the statement made by Morey, he was asked if he thought it was wrong to make such an attack as the one made on Nurse Campbell. Morey stated, "Sort of. I mean I knew it was wrong, but nobody seemed to care."

In his opening statement to the jury, Reading said that although Morey had confessed to the killing of Pauline Campbell, all who had aided, assisted or abetted in the commission of the crime were "equally responsible."

Morey, said Reading, "beat her so hard with the mallet that brain fluid came out" and "the substance of her head splattered the door on a near-by car."

Reading called witnesses to testify, and each recounted what he knew of the crime. Dr. Jack G. Weinbaum, a pathologist at St. Joseph's Mercy Hospital, testified about the autopsy he had performed on the body of Pauline Campbell. He said she had suffered two skull fractures, which had shattered the bones in her head. Dr. Weinbaum said her brain was "torn and crushed and was oozing out" through the skull covering.

Another witness called was Ann Arbor policeman Walter DeDula, the first officer on the scene of the crime. He gave the court a careful description of what he found when he arrived at the Washington Heights residence. DeDula testified to riding in the ambulance with Pauline Campbell. He said she "tried to say something, but couldn't. She just kept mumbling."

The case for the prosecution was soon completed, and it became time for the defense to present its case.

In his opening statement to the jury, defense attorney Ralph C. Keyes said, "This killing is not murder in the first degree." He told the jury that the effects of drinking beer had rendered the three unable to account for their actions.

"Although voluntary drunkenness is no excuse for commission of a crime, nevertheless, where intent is involved, a state of intoxication should be considered in the degree of guilt," said Keyes.

Keyes called William R. Morey III to the stand. Keyes questioned the tall, handsome youth about the night of the murder.

Morey said that on the night in question he went to Pell's house, and then the two went to Ann Arbor to pick up their dates. The four then went to Milan to pick up Royal. After that, they went to a tavern, where Pell purchased a case of beer. Then they went to the west edge of Milan and parked the car near a cornfield. They turned on the radio and began to drink the beer, which was in the back seat of the car.

"If anybody wanted a bottle, they just reached for it. I was drinking rather rapidly," said Morey. He said he drank ten or eleven bottles of beer.

At this point in the story, Morey said his memory of events began to fade. He said he could remember being in the car but was not sure where it was. He could recall taking the dates back to Ann Arbor.

"And do you remember driving around the University Hospital area after taking the girls home?" asked Keyes.

"That's what I've been told," answered Morey.

"Do you remember what happened on Washington Heights?"

Morey answered, "I remember being out of the car…and looking down at something…and Dave was pulling at me."

Keyes questioned Morey about the confession he had signed at Lansing after questioning by police. Morey said he was confused and did not remember what statements he had made. "I would have signed anything to be left alone," said Morey.

Under cross-examination by Reading, Morey was asked, "Is it your claim that you did not kill Miss Campbell?"

"I claim that I do not know for a fact," responded Morey. "I don't remember what happened. I didn't intend to do anything to her."

Reading asked Morey to examine the rubber mallet used in the assault on Nurse Campbell. Morey would not take hold of the mallet. Reading then tossed the mallet into Morey's lap. Morey recoiled from the mallet and brushed it on the courtroom floor.

Next on the witness stand was Pell. Under questioning, Pell admitted to letting Morey out of the car just before Miss Campbell was attacked. Pell said Morey went down the street and out of sight. Pell said he was not following Morey but was looking for him. Pell said he drove onto Washington Heights and saw Morey.

"I stopped the car and asked him what the matter was," said Pell. Morey, said Pell, did not answer but was standing by the street and making a "swinging motion."

Under cross-examination, Reading asked Pell, "Do you claim you're not guilty?"

Pell answered, "Yes." Then he added, "I had something to drink and I didn't know what was happening."

Reading became exasperated with Pell, who answered "I don't know" to many of his questions. Finally, Reading asked Pell, "Is there anything you can say to this jury except 'I don't know?'"

To this question, Pell made no answer.

Royal testified as well. He said he did not know how the three came to be in the University Hospital area.

"Bill said, 'Stop the car…turn off the lights,'" said Royal.

Royal said he saw Morey get out of the car but paid no attention to where he went. He did see, he said, a girl across the sidewalk, with Morey following. Then the two went out of sight. Royal said they went looking for Morey and found him standing beside the curb on Washington Heights.

"I had my window rolled down, and I heard Bill call for help. I first said no, then Max ordered me to get out of the car. I didn't see Bill at first…he was on the other side of the 1951 Ford. I walked to the Ford and saw the girl lying there. He told me to grab hold of one of her arms. I was scared and didn't know what to do. We got to the car, and Bill said to put her in. Max hollered no. I dropped her and jumped into the car."

Near the end of the trial, Prosecutor Reading asked that the rubber mallet and the wrench used in the attacks on nurses be passed to the jury so they could determine the relative weight of each. As Defense Attorney Keyes rose to object, Reading either dropped or tossed the objects onto a table. Keyes accused Reading of doing this so the sound would carry his message to the jury.

Judge Breakey ruled that the evidence could be passed to the jury. He told the members of the jury to decide for themselves if Reading had either accidentally or deliberately dropped the objects on the table. His instructions caused a tittering to be heard from the spectators in the courtroom, some of whom were the same age as Morey, Pell and Royal.

Judge Breakey reprimanded the spectators by saying, "It isn't funny!"

The case went to the jury on November 13, 1951, and after three hours of deliberation, it returned its verdicts. The jury found William Morey and Jacob Max Pell guilty of murder in the first degree and David Royal guilty of murder in the second degree. Judge James Breakey sentenced Morey and Pell to life imprisonment and Royal to twenty-two years in prison.

Sentenced to life in prison, Morey was sent to Jackson Prison. There, he studied French and German, as well as psychology and anthropology, and became an instructor in prison courses and radio-television repair. He was a freelance writer on the magazine market who earned some $10,000. At Jackson, he coordinated the prison inmate blood donor program for almost a decade. All that time, he stayed out of trouble. At Jackson, he had become a model prisoner.

At a parole board hearing in 1970, Morey was asked, "Do you feel remorse?"

He answered, "I do. Yes. Very much so."

After nineteen years in prison, Morey was considered rehabilitated. Michigan governor William Miliken commuted Morey's life sentence on November 25, 1970. Soon after, Morey walked out of prison a free man. He was the last of the three to do so—David Royal had been paroled in 1962, and Max Pell had been paroled in 1967.

After his release, Morey moved to Arizona, where he continued his writing career as the author of children's books. He died in 2005.

13

Panty Raid!

According to legend, the first panty raid—the action of male students at a university storming a women's dormitory to steal items of lingerie—first occurred at the University of Michigan on March 20, 1952. In truth, there had been panty raids before this, but the one at U of M was the raid that started a fad that continued into the early 1960s. For some, the panty raid was harmless fun, a rebellion against the rules restricting the social lives of female students. For others, the raids were a way to burn off pent-up energy and cause some ruckuses. The raids were seen by others as a disruption to educational pursuits. Still, what is perhaps the most famous panty raid did indeed take place on the campus of the University of Michigan on the evening of March 20, 1952.

Winter, with its long, dark nights, gray skies and cold weather, had finally come to an end on that Thursday evening in March. It was the eve of the first day of spring, and the temperature had reached fifty-two degrees. For the first time that year, jackets were left off and windows were opened.

At about 6:30 p.m., Arthur Benford returned to his room after dinner in the Allen Rumsey House in the West Quad of the University of Michigan and attempted to relax by playing his trumpet. His serenade brought an answering trombone blast from the nearby South Quad. The two then entered into a lengthy musical duel. This resulted in shouts of "Knock it off!" Into this mix of noise was added a foghorn and a phonograph playing "Slaughter on Tenth Avenue," which was accompanied by two tubas. All this caused residents to rush out onto Madison Street to sneer at one another. Firecrackers popped as each side shouted threats to the other. By 7:15 p.m., some six hundred young men were facing off on the street.

Neighbors had called police, and a patrol car arrived on the scene. The officers were greeted with catcalls and jeers. The outnumbered officers retreated to their cars, and the students swarmed; some stood on the fenders and rocked the cars.

"The dean will take care of them," said one grim-faced officer.

The Ann Arbor Police Department would keep track of events and had the entire night force on hand. The police watched for property damage and violence. No arrests were made. As one police officer muttered, "What can eight or ten men do against hundreds?"

Then someone shouted, "To the hill!"

The hill meant the girls' dormitories.

At this time, and for years after, the university restricted the social lives of the girls. Women had to be in their dormitories by set hours, and male visitors could only enter the building as far as the lounge. These, and other limits, would remain in force into the 1960s.

The young men swarmed onto State Street, blocking traffic, pounding and rocking cars as they did. The number of the men grew as more joined the fun. At Betsy Barbour and Helen Newberry Halls, the men heckled residents and broke into the lounges. The men then moved on to North University. At Stockwell Hall, the men swarmed into the lounge and then made their way to Mosher-Jordan. The next stop was the Alice Lloyd Hall, where the women were prepared. The front doors were locked, blocking the entrance of the men for a time. As some of the men pounded on the front doors and yelled, others went to the side doors of the dorm, rushed up the stairs and spread out through the top floors. As the men ran through the halls, some picked up panties—or what the *Ann Arbor News* called "miscellaneous female unmentionables." The front doors of the hall somehow were opened, and the waiting men rushed into the lounge.

The men turned from the hall and made their way to the Michigan League, where the Junior Girls' play was being performed. The men tried to enter the league but were stopped by locked doors.

Some of the men left the campus and made their way to the Michigan Theater, forced their way into the theater and ran onto the stage, where they sang a chorus or two of "The Victors." This action was during a showing of the movie *Behave Yourself.*

Then came the counterattack. Chanting women marched from Observatory Hill and made their way to the Michigan Union. At this time, women were not allowed to enter the union unless escorted by a male. The women forced their way through the front doors of the union and ambled through the building at will.

Next, the women moved on to West Quad, where surprised residents were caught with their shorts on. These guys had to run for safety. Here, it is said, some of the women picked up a few souvenirs of their own.

"In West Quad," reported the *Michigan Daily* on March 22, 1952, "during the coed counter-attack, a resident advisor, who is also an instructor, spied one of his women students parading through a third floor corridor. She greeted him by sticking out her tongue, and then fled down the corridor."

From West Quad, the women moved on to South Quad, where some men formed a barrier at the front doors, while others beckoned them on. The screaming women broke through the barrier and entered the lounge. The lounge became a cluttered mess in minutes as staff hysterically called the men to order. The rush of the women to the top floor was stopped by dean of women Deborah Bacon, who rounded up the girls and sent them back to their dorms.

To reporters, Dean Bacon said, "Well, boys will be boys."

Dean Bacon then hurried to Mosher Hall, where the boys were running through the corridors. Soon after Dean Bacon arrived, the boys headed out.

Now the boys headed toward Alice Lloyd Hall, spurred on by a flashing red light in one of the windows. To the women lining the windows, the boys yelled, "Water, water!" Women filled wastebaskets with water and tossed the water out the windows. Sometimes, the water was tossed out the window while still in the basket.

"After futile attempts to crash the large front doors into the main lounge of the Hall, a few enterprising males climbed up on the roof and jumped through open windows, to the horror of surprised residents," noted the *Michigan Daily* of Friday, March 21, 1952.

"While housemothers looked on half-smilingly," continued the account, "a steady stream of yelling students piled into the top floors and ran rampant through the corridors. Some invaded women's rooms and escaped to the outdoors waving unmentionables."

The men moved on to Couzens Hall, where they were stopped by locked doors. A staff member opened the front portal; as she later explained, "I thought it was good psychology."

"After a brief tour of Couzens," noted the *Michigan Daily*, "the crowd gathered momentum again with cries of 'On to Victor Vaughn!' The Vaughan invasion proved to be the turning point when, after a thorough survey of the dorm's interior, the mob was quieted by a resigned Dean Bacon who soberly told members of the group the fun was over."

"As the remnants of the once boisterous crew straggled toward State St.," the account continued, "the dean walked toward a waiting car whistling in the face of a battery of photographers."

During the raid on Vaughan, a man entered a room with suitcase in hand and told the coed that he was her new roommate and asked where he could stow his stuff.

The body of men now stormed Martha Cook and entered the building through a side door. They marched up and down the corridors, raising havoc. Four doors were broken in the building.

At this point, about 10:30 p.m., university president Harlan Hatcher emerged from his home and told the men to "go back to your dorms." Some did; some did not.

At about midnight, a group of men stormed Betsy Barbour, where the women used a fire hose to cool their high spirits.

The panty raid came to a complete end at about 1:15 a.m., when rain began to fall.

"The student demonstration was a form of spring madness," said dean of students Erich A. Walter in a statement. "The term 'madness' has the implication of being something uncontrollable. We were fortunate in not having serious accidents, in not having a mob spirit develop. I am glad that there had to be no arrests and that property damage was of an insignificant character."

"I am sorry that a few of our students showed some pretty bad manners," noted Dean Walter,

> *most of them, considering that they were out of order, showed marks of self-control which, in general are the characteristics of our student body.*

> *If any students are reported to us who have violated specific University regulations, these students will be heard by the regularly constituted disciplinary authorities.*
>
> *In reviewing the demonstration, we obviously shall try to establish some controls of a moral character that may operate in a crisis. Obviously, this is difficult to accomplish. No human being has ever attempted to shift the vernal equinox.*

Once the event had passed, there came the task of explaining what had happened and why it had happened. Most agreed that the warm weather had something to do with it. Others pointed out that students were feeling tension from approaching mid-semester and suggested this, with spring weather, as a cause.

Professor Guy E. Swanson of the Sociology Department noted that spring and mid-semester had come at this time of year before but student riots had not.

"As nearly as we can tell," added Professor Amos Hawley of the Sociology Department, "one of the salient points was the arrival of police on the scene. Up to then it was a usual sort of thing, but that gave it a rallying point and set up a conflict situation."

Professor Roger Heyns of the Psychology Department felt the question of why this had happened should not be dropped after a few casual guesses. "If I were sitting in the administrative position I'd certainly find out positively. I'd like to know whether I was sitting on a powder keg or whether I was just surrounded by normal, wholesome American boys."

Professor Frank Grace of the political science department said the events "seemed to knock the pins from under Rousseau's theory of the nobleness of man in a state of nature."

Finally, there was the Victor Vaughan resident who said, "I don't care why they started it; I think it's the most fun we've had all year."

14

Strange Disappearance of Cheng Lim

Cheng Lim was feeling depressed in the fall of 1955, as he felt he had failed the people who had sponsored him. A native of Singapore, Cheng Lim came to the University of Michigan in 1952 as a transfer student from Albion College. He enrolled in the College of Engineering and at first made good grades. His sponsoring agency was the Methodist Church, which had brought him to America and helped him with tuition and living expenses. He received additional aid from other foreign students, who were members of the Wesley Foundation. Reluctant to accept the aid, he promised to repay the loans as soon as he could.

During the fall of 1954, he had trouble with mathematics and his physics courses. At the end of the semester, he had failed two courses. His money was gone, and he decided not to ask his friends for more money. Lim did not enroll for classes when the fall semester began.

"So many people helped me," said Lim later. "I failed them all. I just couldn't face them."

On October 8, 1955, the day of the University of Michigan–Navy game, Lim walked down to the Huron River. There, in an attempt to fake his suicide, he tossed his passport into the water. Later that night, he walked to the First Methodist Church at State and Huron Streets. It was almost dark, so there was no one around.

Lim had done janitorial work at the church, so he knew the building well. He climbed a ladder that led to the attic on the north side of the church. He found several boards and lay these across the flooring rafters of the loft. On the boards, he placed an old church seat cushion. Then he went to slept.

This was the start of Cheng Lim's self-imposed exile. For the next four years, he would hear voices but would never speak to anyone. He would remain in hiding, never leaving the church building.

"The first days I was acting on my reflexes," he later recalled. "I heard the children playing and the students walking back and forth to classes. I wanted to go to them, to be with them, to talk with them. I couldn't."

Each night, Lim slipped down from the attic to the kitchen to look for food left by the church groups. Sometimes he ate well, and sometimes he went for days with nothing to eat. He bathed himself in the church restrooms and filled a pitcher with water to keep him supplied for the next day. He brushed his teeth with matchsticks and trimmed his hair with a pair of shears. He found a length of rope, and in the early morning hours, he would skip rope in the lounge section of the church.

When he thought he was close to having a mental breakdown, Lim would enter a downstairs closet with a heavy, sound-deadening door. There, he would sing at the top of his voice and shout and scream until he felt better.

Every night, he visited the church library. To keep his mind active, he would read every magazine and every pamphlet and booklet. *Time* magazine arrived every Wednesday, and Lim read it cover to cover.

His nights in the church were not bad, but for Lim, the days were very hard.

"I knew someone would hear me while they worked downstairs in the daytime if I moved around," he later explained. "I would just lie on my mat, very still, all day long. In the summer, it would get very hot from the roof above me. I believe it got about 115 degrees many times."

The winters were almost as bad, with the wind cutting through the cracks in the rafters. Snow drifted into his hiding place. The cold bit at his hands and feet. He sewed two blankets together and wrapped them around him. There were days when he could not sleep because of the cold.

Lim's friends reported him missing to university authorities a week after he hid himself in the church. Unable to find Lim, university officials turned the case over to the police. Police issued an all-points bulletin, listing Lim as a missing person, on November 29, 1955. Walter B. Rea, the dean of men at the university, and the Reverend Eugene A. Ransom kept in touch with Lim's brother in Canada and his sister in England. Neither had any idea of where Lim was. Reverend Ransom sometimes wondered what had become of Lim, having no idea that he was hiding in the attic almost directly above his office.

Members of the church noticed that food was missing from the kitchen. In about June 1959, a woman arrived at the church at 6:00 a.m. to prepare food for a banquet. She pushed open a door to the kitchen to see a shadowy figure standing at a table. He was wearing a small hat, gloves, rumpled pants and a dark shirt. The woman screamed and fled the kitchen. Lim ran to the attic. Six police officers searched the church but found nothing. Lim crouched between the rafters of the attic, shaken and frightened, but safe.

Over the years, the Ann Arbor Police Department received a number of calls concerning a prowler in the church. Each time, the police searched the church but found nothing. Caretakers lived in the basement of the church and sometimes heard footsteps on the first floor when Lim was gathering food. Finally, the church employed a security guard as concerns grew.

William Edison was a night patrolman for the Sanford Security Agency on the night of August 30, 1959, when he heard a footstep. He called the police, and Officers Norman Olmstead and Ritchie Davis responded to the call. The two searched the church, walking through almost every room in the building. They saw no trace of a prowler. They finished their search at about 5:30 a.m. As the two officers turned to leave, Officer Olmstead stopped in his tracks. Out of the corner of his eye, he had seen a steel door at the top of a ladder-type stairway move.

Olmstead said to Davis, "Let's check up above, Ritchie."

They climbed the steel staircase and then climbed out on to the flat roof above the north wing of the church. They walked across the roof to a door to the rafter section.

Opening the door, the officers flashed their lights down the forty-foot-long space. Peering in, the two officers saw Lim's bed, a jar of instant coffee and a box of crackers. The officers entered the space and began to look around, Olmstead on one side and Davis on the other. Davis turned the beam of his light down a four-foot hole in the packed insulation near the eaves. There, rolled into a ball, his head down and arms under him, was Lim.

Davis called to Olmstead, "I don't see anybody here."

From the way Davis spoke, Olmstead concluded that he had seen something. Then, Olmstead heard Davis draw his weapon from his holster. As Davis leveled his revolver, he called out, "Come out with your hands up! Quick!"

Lim stood up with his hands in the air.

To the officers, Lim's appearance was just wild. Stripped to the waist, he wore a pair of old swimming trunks. On his head, Lim wore a rimless cap from which his long hair seemed to flare out. His coppery body glistened with sweat.

The officers placed Lim's hands behind his back and handcuffed him.

At the station, Lim told his story of hiding in the church for four years.

Lim had kept his wristwatch. Every morning he had wound his watch, but over the years the watch began to lose time. The watch had been an hour slow during the last year.

"But when I went downstairs each night I set it by the church clocks," Lim told Lieutenant Harold E. Olson of the Ann Arbor Police Department. Lieutenant Olson was the first officer to question Lim.

"What did you care about the time?" asked Olson. "Time meant nothing to you."

"Oh, but it did," answered Lim. "Time and how it passed became part of my living pattern."

"Police bluntly said they found Cheng's story hard to believe," reported the *Ypsilanti Press* of Monday, August 31, 1959. "On the other hand, they said they had no definite reason to doubt him either."

The next morning, Lim, now dressed in a gray suit, white shirt, gray tie and sneakers, held a press conference in the Ann Arbor City Council chambers. He told the thirty reporters that he had learned that morning that his father died of cancer the previous February in Singapore.

"That makes it very hard for me, you see," said Lim. He blinked his eyes several times. "That was just six months ago."

The same day as the press conference, police released Lim to agents of the United States Immigration Service, who took him to a local restaurant and treated him to lunch. He was then taken to the International Center, where he was released on parole to Robert B. Klinger, counselor for foreign students.

The next day, September 1, 1959, Lim underwent a complete physical, which found him to be in surprisingly good condition. His muscle tone was good, and his teeth were in fair condition. The doctors noted that he had received adequate amounts of three key vitamins: A, C and D.

"A person who goes without these vitamins for any length of time will become rundown and very ill," explained one of the doctors. "This man seemed to have had plenty of these during his seclusion."

A university graduate opened a savings account for Lim. He did this, although he did not know Lim, because he believed Lim had suffered a "terrible miscarriage of human understanding." The graduate, who chose to remain anonymous, explained, "I simply figured Lim will need money whether he stays here or leaves the country. I paid my way through school and know what it means to need money."

Lim decided to return to the University of Michigan and complete his education. This decision was made after Lim talked with his mother by telephone, and she encouraged him to continue his studies. He was eligible for readmission with the standing of a junior, Clyde Vroman, director of admissions, explained to the *Ann Arbor News* of Wednesday, September 2, 1959. He added that no special provisions were made for Lim to be readmitted.

"If Lim had asked for a transfer from the engineering school in the spring of 1955, he would have been transferred," explained Vroman. "This student never flunked out. He was simply on probation."

Lim graduated in 1961 and returned to Singapore. He died of a heart attack in the 1970s.

Bibliography

Beakes, Samuel W. *Past and Present of Washtenaw County Michigan.* N.p: S.J. Clark Publishing Co., 1906.

Chapman, Charles C. *History of Washtenaw County Michigan.* Chicago: Charles C. Chapman & Co., 1881.

Dangers of Drink

Probable Murder

Ann Arbor Journal. "Probable Murder." November 6, 1861.

Michigan Argus. "The Late Murder." November 15, 1861.

———. "Probable Murder." November 8, 1861.

Michigan State News. Inquisition on the dead body of John Innis. November 12, 1861.

Death of O'Brien

Detroit Free Press. "A Man Named William O'Brien Murdered." October 11, 1869.

———. "The Murder of William O'Brien." October 13, 1869.

Michigan Argus. "A Murder in Our City." October 15, 1869.
Ypsilanti Commercial. "Drunkenness and Licentiousness." October 9, 1869.

Shooting Affray

Michigan Argus, November 18, 1879; December 2, 1870.
———. "Shooting Affray." November 4, 1870.
Peninsular Courier, November 4, 1870; November 18, 1870; March 10, 1871.

Fatal Row at Flannary's Saloon

Michigan Argus. "Fatal Saloon Row." November 6, 1874.
Peninsular Courier. "Murder of Richard Flannary." November 6, 1874.

DOUBLE MURDER

Detroit Free Press, October 26, 1871.
Michigan Argus. "A Horrible Murder." October 27, 1871.
———. "The Trial of Wagner." March 15, 1872.
Peninsular Courier. "Double Murder." October 27, 1871.

DEFALCATION AT THE UNIVERSITY

Peckham, Howard H. *The Making of the University of Michigan.* Ann Arbor: University of Michigan Press, 1967.

The Regents of the University of Michigan v. Preston B. Rose, Silas H. Douglas, Rice Beal and William B. Smith. Harvey S. Street and John Q. Wilson, executors—Original bill, *Silas H. Douglas, appellant, v. The Regents of the University of Michigan*—Cross bill. Brief on behalf of Silas H. Douglas, appellant. Sam'l T. Douglas, solicitor for appellant, Ashley Pound, of counsel.

The Regents of the University of Michigan v. Preston B. Rose, Silas H. Douglas, Rice Beal, et al. Michigan Reports. In *Cases Decided of the Supreme Court of Michigan*, Vol. 45. Chicago: Gallaghan &Co, 1882

Smith, Shirley W. *James Burrill Angell...an American Influence*. Ann Arbor: University of Michigan Press, 1954.

Velde, Lewis G. Vander. *The Douglas-Rose Controversy*. Encyclopedic Survey, vol. I. Ann Arbor: University of Michigan, n.d.

DEATH OF A STUDENT

Ann Arbor Argus. "Killed with a Musket." November 14, 1890.

Ann Arbor Courier. "Ann Arbor Excited!" November 19, 1890.

Detroit Evening News. "Ann Arbor's Murder." November 14, 1890.

———. "One Student Killed." November 13, 1890.

———. "President Angell Is Silent." November 17, 1890.

———. "The University Riot." November 14, 1890.

———. "Who Killed Dennison." November 15, 1890.

Detroit Free Press. "Something Like a Riot." November 13, 1890.

JACK THE HUGGER

Ann Arbor Courier-Register. "A Bold Hold Up." January 30, 1901.

———. "Jack the Hugger Has Been Located." October 7, 1903.

Ann Arbor Daily Argus. "Struck Her with His Fist." October 14, 1901.

Evening Times. "Jack the Hugger." January 4, 1900.

———. "Jack the Hugger Has Been Located." October 3, 1903.

Washtenaw Times, January 29, 1901; October 15, 1901.

Ypsilanti Commercial. "Jack the Hugger." January 11, 1900.

DIME NOVEL DISAPPEARANCE OF ALBERT PATTERSON

Ann Arbor Argus. "Mysterious Disappearance with Possible Murder." May 21, 1903.

Ann Arbor Daily Argus. "Is Patterson Still Living?" August 6, 1903.

———. "It Was Blood on the Hat." May 23, 1903.

———. "No Blood Was on the Hat." May 22, 1903.

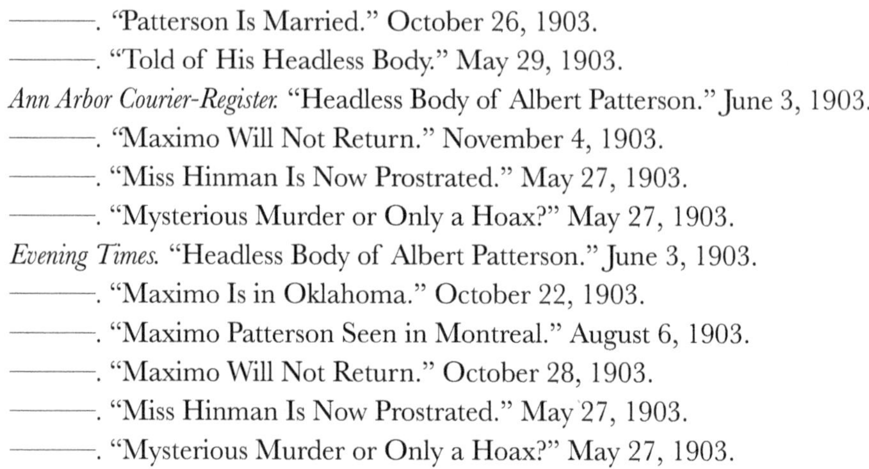
———. "Patterson Is Married." October 26, 1903.
———. "Told of His Headless Body." May 29, 1903.
Ann Arbor Courier-Register. "Headless Body of Albert Patterson." June 3, 1903.
———. "Maximo Will Not Return." November 4, 1903.
———. "Miss Hinman Is Now Prostrated." May 27, 1903.
———. "Mysterious Murder or Only a Hoax?" May 27, 1903.
Evening Times. "Headless Body of Albert Patterson." June 3, 1903.
———. "Maximo Is in Oklahoma." October 22, 1903.
———. "Maximo Patterson Seen in Montreal." August 6, 1903.
———. "Maximo Will Not Return." October 28, 1903.
———. "Miss Hinman Is Now Prostrated." May 27, 1903.
———. "Mysterious Murder or Only a Hoax?" May 27, 1903.

Riot at the Star Theatre

Ann Arbor Daily Times. "Bail Was Secured by Accused Student." March 18, 1908.
———. "The Dawn of Peace." March 27, 1908.
———. "Disgraceful Riot at Star Theatre." March 17, 1908
———. "Examination Continues." March 23, 1908.
———. "General Movement to Help Arrest Men." March 19, 1908.
———. "Hearing Is on in Riot Case." March 23, 1908.
———. "Riot Cases Were Put Over." March 26, 1908.
———. "Students Decide to Pay for all Damages Done." March 18, 1908.
Ann Arbor News-Argus. "Adjourned until Monday." March 20, 1908.
———. "And All the Rest Waived." March 27, 1908.
———. "Chief Apfel on the Stand." March 24, 1908.
———. "Fifteen Students Handcuffed." March 17, 1908.
———. "First Student Bound Over." March 25, 1908.
———. "It Is Anarchy Says Justice Doty." March 19, 1908.
———. "Mayor Sends in a Letter." March 26, 1908.
———. "A Petition for Their Release." March 21, 1908.
———. "Students' Petition and Citizens Who Signed." March 24, 1908.
———. "Two More Students Arrested Last Night." March 18, 1908.
Detroit News. "15 University Students Face Charge of Riot." March 17, 1908.

Detroit Free Press. "2,000 Students Wreck Nickel Theater." March 17, 1908.
Michigan Daily "Crowd raids Star theatre" Tuesday, March 17, 1908
———. "Filthy Hole Bears Name of County Jail." March 18, 1908.
Peckham, Howard H. *The Making of the University of Michigan.* Ann Arbor: University of Michigan Press, 1967.
Sagendorph, Kent. *Michigan: The Story of the University.* New York: E.P. Dutton & Co.., 1948.
Smith, Shirley W. *Harry Burns Hutchins and the University of Michigan.* Ann Arbor: University of Michigan Press, 1951.
———. *James Burrill Angell…an American Influence.* Ann Arbor: University of Michigan Press, 1954.

Mystery Surrounds Death of Foster Campbell

Ann Arbor Daily Times News. "Adjourns Inquest Indefinitely." January 25, 1911.
———. "New Angle to Mystery." January 21, 1911.
———. "Murder or Suicide?" January 20, 1911.
Ypsilanti Daily Press. "Lad of 9 Years Found Dead with Rope on His Neck." January 20, 1911.
———. "Theories as to Cause of Lad's Death Differ." January 21, 1911.

Police Raid Fraternities

Ann Arbor Daily News. "Liquor Seized in Raids on Fraternities." February 11, 1931.
Washtenaw Tribune. "Campus Booze Vendors Get Severe Terms." February 23, 1931.
———. "84 Students Told to Report after Liquor Raids." February 13, 1931.
———. "M committee May Reconsider Padlocking." February 16, 1931.
———. "M committee Stands Pat on Closing Frats." February 20, 1931.
Ypsilanti Daily Press. "80 Students Caught in U Frat Liquor Raid." February 11, 1931.
———. "Frat Discipline May Be Lessened in Meeting Today." February 16, 1931.

———. "Fraternity Boys Face No Charges." February 20, 1931.
———. "Frat Punishment Held too Severe." February 14, 1931.
———. "Frats in Liquor Scandal Closed for Six Months." February 13, 1931.
———. "U Student Discipline Considered." February 12, 1931.

BETTY BAKER GOES ON TRIAL

Ann Arbor News. "Betty Baker Stands Mute." October 6, 1936.
———. "Betty Baker Tells Story of Friendship." January 7, 1937.
———. "Evidence in Baker Trial Is Started." January 5, 1937.
———. "Judge Assigns Life Sentence to Mrs. Baker." January 13, 1937.
———. "Jury to Get Baker Case Late Today." January 12, 1937.
———. "Mrs. Betty Baker Held to Circuit Court without Bond." July 9, 1936.
———. "Murder Trial Is Adjourned until Monday." January 9, 1937.
———. "Murder Trial of Mrs. Betty Baker Slated to Start." N.d.
———. "Rapp Fails to Change Story of Mrs. Baker." January 8, 1937.
———. "States Divorce Was Intended by Mrs. Baker." January 6, 1937.
———. "Woman Faces Arraignment Here Today." July 1, 1936.
———. "Woman Starts Life Sentence." January 14, 1937.
Detroit Free Press. "Dancer's Case May Be Given to Jury Today." January 12, 1937.
———. "Didn't Intend to Killer Lover, Dancer Holds." January 8, 1937.
———. "Doctor Admits Telling Dancer the Way to Kill." January 7, 1937.
———. "Eyes Opened in Court Room, Baker Admits." January 10, 1937.
———. "Life Term Is Given to Betty Baker in Murder of Lover." January 13, 1937.
———. "State Witness Helps Dancer in Death Trial." January 6, 1937.
Detroit News. "Betty Baker Tells Story." January 7, 1937.
———. "Husband on Witness Stand Defends His Wife in Slaying." January 9, 1937.
———. "Killer Bares Love Affair." January 8, 1937.
———. "Wife Calls Slaying an Accident." January 5, 1937.
———. "Witness Calls Killer Jealous." January 6, 1937.
Ypsilanti Daily Press. "Work Assigned for Mrs. Baker." January 15, 1937.

Ann Arbor Police Gambling Scandal

Ann Arbor News. "Accused Police Heads Suspended; Chief Will Fight." June 12, 1946.

———. "Attorneys Clash on Progress in Police Hearings." August 9, 1946.

———. "Breakey Asks Removal of Police Chief." June 11, 1946.

———. "Gehringer Denies Taking Any Bribes." August 13, 1946.

———. "Mortenson Cleared, Gehringer Fired." August 22, 1946.

———. "Mortenson Denies Protecting Gambling." August 10, 1946.

———. "Mortenson Resigns as Chief of Police." August 6, 1946.

———. "Police Board Told of Bets Being Placed." August 7, 1946.

———. "Prosecution Nears End in Police Case." August 7, 1946.

———. "Text of Police Commission's Report." August 22, 1946.

———. "Witness Fails to Testify on Bribe Charge." August 8, 1946.

Logghe, Michael. Ann Arbor Police Department Online History Exhibit. Ann Arbor District Library website.

Death of a Nurse

Ann Arbor News. "Boy Who Killed Nurse Termed 'Jekyll and Hyde' Case." September 20, 1951.

———. "Defense Lawyers Rest Their Case in Murder Trial." November 9, 1951.

———. "Escort Service Provided Nurses Following Killing." September 18, 1951.

———. "Lawyer Says Morey Will Take Stand." November 6, 1951.

———. "Morey Says He Does Not Recall Part in Slaying." November 7, 1951.

———. "Nurse Brutally Slain Here." September 17, 1951.

———. "Police Still without Clue to Slaying." September 19, 1951.

———. "Prosecution Case All but Over as Trial Adjourns." November 3, 1951.

———. "Psychiatrist Says Killer May Repeat if 'Psychotic.'" September 18, 1951.

———. "Reading Asks First Degree Jury Verdicts." November 13, 1951.

———. "Royal Testifies Morey Warned Against 'Telling.'" November 8, 1951.

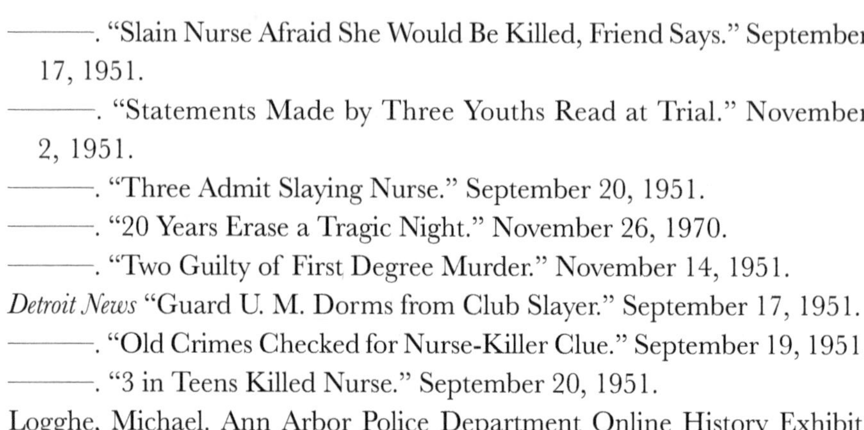

———. "Slain Nurse Afraid She Would Be Killed, Friend Says." September 17, 1951.

———. "Statements Made by Three Youths Read at Trial." November 2, 1951.

———. "Three Admit Slaying Nurse." September 20, 1951.

———. "20 Years Erase a Tragic Night." November 26, 1970.

———. "Two Guilty of First Degree Murder." November 14, 1951.

Detroit News "Guard U. M. Dorms from Club Slayer." September 17, 1951.

———. "Old Crimes Checked for Nurse-Killer Clue." September 19, 1951.

———. "3 in Teens Killed Nurse." September 20, 1951.

Logghe, Michael. Ann Arbor Police Department Online History Exhibit. Ann Arbor District Library website.

Panty Raid!

Ann Arbor News. "Students Greet Spring in Noisy Demonstration." March 21, 1952.

Detroit News. "Coed's Fire Hose Ends Riotous Night at U of M." March 21, 1952.

Michigan Daily. "Campus Regard Riot Causes." March 22, 1952.

———."Mass Riot Rocks Campus." March 21, 1952.

———. "Trumpet Triggers Trouble." March 22, 1952.

Strange Disappearance of Cheng Lim

Ann Arbor News. "Church Recluse Decides to Complete Education." September 2, 1952.

———. "Hides Four Years in Church Rafters." N.d.

———. "Lim's Health Good Hospital Tests Show." September 1, 1959.

Detroit Free Press. "4 Years in an Attic." August 31, 1959.

Detroit News. "U-M Flunker Hides Out 4 Years in Church Attic." August 31, 1959.

Logghe, Michael. Ann Arbor Police Department Online History Exhibit. Ann Arbor District Library website.

About the Author

James Thomas Mann is a local historian, storyteller and author in Ypsilanti. His books include *Ypsilanti: A History in Pictures*; *Ypsilanti in the 20th Century*; *City of Ypsilanti Fire Department 100 Years*; *Footnotes in History*; and *Our Heritage: Down by the Depot in Ypsilanti* with Tom Dodd. His previous book with The History Press was *Wicked Washtenaw County*.

www.ingramcontent.com/pod-product-compliance
Lightning Source LLC
LaVergne TN
LVHW010950100826
845153LV00002B/192
9781540230539